One Kid at a Time

Mentor Handbook

OTHER YOUTH SPECIALTIES TITLES

PROFESSIONAL RESOURCES

The Church and the American Teenager
  (previously released as Growing Up in America)
Developing Spiritual Growth in Junior High Students
Equipped to Serve
Help! I'm a Sunday School Teacher!
Help! I'm a Volunteer Youth Worker!
High School Ministry
How to Recruit and Train Volunteer Youth Workers
  (previously released as Unsung Heroes)
Junior High Ministry (Revised Edition)
The Ministry of Nurture
Peer Counseling in Youth Groups
Advanced Peer Counseling in Youth Groups
The Youth Minister's Survival Guide
Youth Ministry Nuts and Bolts

DISCUSSION STARTER RESOURCES

Amazing Tension Getters
Get 'Em Talking
High School TalkSheets
Junior High TalkSheets
High School TalkSheets: Psalms and Proverbs
Junior High TalkSheets: Psalms and Proverbs
More High School TalkSheets
More Junior High TalkSheets
Option Plays
Parent Ministry TalkSheets
Tension Getters
Tension Getters Two
Would You Rather . . . ?

IDEAS LIBRARY

Ideas Combo 1-4, 5-8, 9-12, 13-16, 17-20, 21-24, 25-28,
  29-32, 33-36, 37-40, 41-44, 45-48, 49-52, 53, 54
Ideas Index

YOUTH MINISTRY PROGRAMMING

Adventure Games
Compassionate Kids
Creative Bible Lessons
Creative Programming Ideas for Junior High Ministry
Creative Socials and Special Events
Dramatic Pauses
Facing Your Future
Great Fundraising Ideas for Youth Groups
Great Games for City Kids
Great Ideas for Small Youth Groups
Great Retreats for Youth Groups
Greatest Skits on Earth
Greatest Skits on Earth, Volume 2
Holiday Ideas for Youth Groups (Revised Edition)
Hot Illustrations for Youth Talks
Hot Talks
Junior High Game Nights

More Junior High Game Nights
On-Site: 40 On-Location Youth Programs
Play It! Great Games for Groups
Play It Again! More Great Games for Groups
Road Trip
Super Sketches for Youth Ministry
Teaching the Bible Creatively
Teaching the Truth About Sex
Up Close and Personal: How to Build Community in
  Your Youth Group

4TH-6TH GRADE MINISTRY

Attention Grabbers for 4th-6th Graders
4th-6th Grade TalkSheets
Great Games for 4th-6th Graders
How to Survive Middle School
Incredible Stories
More Attention Grabbers for 4th-6th Graders
More Great Games for 4th-6th Graders
Quick and Easy Activities for 4th-6th Graders
More Quick and Easy Activities for 4th-6th Graders
Teach 'Toons

CLIP ART

ArtSource Volume 1—Fantastic Activities
ArtSource Volume 2—Borders, Symbols, Holidays, and
  Attention Getters
ArtSource Volume 3—Sports
ArtSource Volume 4—Phrases and Verses
ArtSource Volume 5—Amazing Oddities and Appalling Images
ArtSource Volume 6—Spiritual Topics
Youth Specialties Clip Art Book
Youth Specialties Clip Art Book, Volume 2

VIDEO

Edge TV
God Views
The Heart of Youth Ministry: A Morning with Mike Yaconelli
Next Time I Fall in Love Video Curriculum
Promo Spots for Junior High Game Nights
Resource Seminar Video Series
Understanding Your Teenager Video Curriculum
Witnesses

STUDENT BOOKS

Going the Distance
Grow for It Journal
Grow for It Journal Through the Scriptures
How to Live with Your Parents Without Losing Your Mind
I Don't Remember Dropping the Skunk, But I Do Remember
  Trying to Breathe
Next Time I Fall in Love
Next Time I Fall in Love Journal
101 Things to Do During a Dull Sermon

OTHER DAVID C. COOK TITLES

CUSTOM CURRICULUM

Basic Training
Beliefs to Beware Of
The Big Screen
Bouncing Back
Can't Help It?
Extreme Closeup
Face to Face with Jesus
Free Gifts for Everybody!
Going against the Flow
Gotta Have It?
Hormone Helper
In the Beginning . . . What?
Is Anybody There?
Just Look at You!
Next Stop: High School
N.T. Speedway
O.T. Speedway
Parent Pains
Riding Those Mood Swings
Streetwise
They're Not Like Us!
Tongue Untwisters
Too Tough?
Unseen Mysteries
What Do You Think?
What, Me Holy?
What Would Jesus Do?
Which Way to God?
The Whole Story
Why Be a Christian?
Your Bible's Alive!
You've Got Style!

FIRST AID FOR YOUTH GROUPS

When Kids Are Apathetic
When Kids Are Touched by Crisis
When Kids Aren't Close
When Kids Ask Sticky Questions
When Kids Ask More Sticky Questions
When Kids Don't Know the Basics
When Kids Have Personal Problems
When Kids Have More Personal Problems

GREAT GROUPS

Families in Flux Journal
Families in Flux Leader's Guide
Who Am I? Journal
Who Am I? Leader's Guide
The First Family Tree Bible Study Journal
The First Family Tree Leader's Guide
Gospel on the Go Bible Study Journal
Gospel on the Go Leader's Guide
Never the Same Disciple's Journal
Never the Same Leader's Guide
No Turning Back Disciple's Journal
No Turning Back Leader's Guide

HOT TOPICS YOUTH ELECTIVES

Dating, College Prep, and a Reason to Live
Money, Creation and Evolution, and Temptation
Music, Friends and Enemies, and Church Complaints
Peer Pressure, Other Religions, and Jobs and Careers
School, Male and Female, and Doubts
Self-Image, Drugs and Alcohol, and More Tough Questions
Sports, Family Trouble, and Tough Questions
TV and Movies, Feelings, and the Future

INCREDIBLE MEETING MAKERS

Listen Up!
Look It Up!
Mix It Up!
Talk It Up!
Team Up!
Wrap It Up!

JUNIOR ELECTIVES

Families, The Environment, Sports and Competition
Growing as a Christian, School, Leisure Time
My Body, Divorce, The Occult
My Future, Feelings, Stewardship
Peer Pressure, Pain and Death, Heroes
Problems in Society, Making Choices, Friendship
Self-Esteem, Differences, Authority
Substance Abuse, Communicating with Others, Who Is Jesus?

JUNIOR HIGHS ONLY

Good Times!
Grow Up!
I Believe!
Some People!
That Hurts!
That's Life!
That's Me!
Watch Out!

QUICK STUDIES B.C./QUICK STUDIES

Genesis—Deuteronomy
Joshua—Esther
Job—Song of Songs
Isaiah—Malachi
Matthew & Mark
Luke & John
Acts & Romans
I Corinthians—Ephesians
Philippians—Hebrews
James—Revelation

SNAP SESSIONS

Celebrations & Choice Makers
Everyday Issues & Fellowship Builders
Fun Nights & Faith Builders
Holiday Specials & Boredom Busters
Popular Passages & Spiritual Challenges
Skill Builders & Problem Solvers

One Kid at a Time
Mentor Handbook

Miles McPherson
with
Wayne Rice

Youth
Specialties

El Cajon, California

David C. Cook Publishing Co.
Colorado Springs, CO/Paris, Ontario

One Kid at a Time: Mentor Handbook

Copyright © 1995 by Youth Specialties, Inc.

Youth Specialties Books, 1224 Greenfield Drive, El Cajon, California 92021,
are published by David C. Cook Church Ministry Resources,
a division of Cook Communications Ministries International,
Colorado Springs, CO 80918

Unless otherwise noted, Scripture quotations are from the Holy Bible, New International Version (NIV), © 1973, 1978, 1984 by International Bible Society. Used by permission of Zondervan Bible Publishers.

Edited by Noel Becchetti, Randy Southern, and Pam Campbell
Typography and Design by Patton Brothers Design

Printed in the United States of America

ISBN: 0-7814-5205-8

Library of Congress Catalog Number: 95-61010

94 95 96 97 98 99/ /6 5 4 3 2 1

TABLE OF CONTENTS

Introduction

CONGRATULATIONS! YOU'RE A MENTOR! One of the greatest honors that we have as human beings is to be someone else's mentor. A mentor is a person who is permitted to provide guidance and direction for someone who is younger or less experienced. The word *mentor* was first used in Homer's *The Odyssey*. It was a person's name. Mentor was entrusted with the education of his friend Odysseus's son Telemachus. He was more than a teacher or tutor to Telemachus, however. He was a constant companion and friend who completely committed himself completely to the health and well-being of his young charge. Today, the idea of mentoring implies the same kind of relationship. A mentor is someone who enters a voluntary relationship of trust and mutual respect with another person, in which learning happens as a byproduct. Put another way, mentoring has more to do with *who you are* than *what you do.*

If this were a book about teaching, we could prescribe a certain method for teaching and give you the materials with which to do it. However, mentoring is not teaching. There is no particular method for mentoring. Everyone is different, and how you mentor a young person will be different from how anyone else does it. Your view of mentoring is shaped by your personality, your gifts and abilities, and your own personal experience. All of us have had mentors in our lives—people we admired and learned from. How you remember the mentors in your life will help determine the kind of mentor that you will become.

The primary job of a mentor is to come alongside a young person and simply *be there* for him or her. *Being there* doesn't require a master's degree in education or a lot of experience in youth work. All it requires is the willingness to get to know one young person and the time to actually do it. After that, mentoring pretty much takes care of itself. You will have opportunities to influence and guide your young person in many ways, whether you are engaged in a serious discussion about life or just having fun.

This book will help you get the most from your mentoring experience. It doesn't tell you everything you need to know about mentoring, but it does contain some good ideas to stimulate your own creativity. Mentoring, like most important things in life, cannot be done by following an instruction manual. Use this book as a tool to cultivate your own style of mentoring—one that will uniquely benefit both you and the young person you are mentoring.

If you feel unqualified to be a mentor, that's good. More often than not, people who are highly qualified make lousy mentors. Usually, when God wants to get something important done, He tends to call on people who are reluctant to do it (see Moses, Abraham, Isaiah, Paul, and others). God looks for people who must depend on Him for help, not people who think they can do it on their own. If you have a desire to serve God and a desire to have a positive influence on a young person, then you can be a mentor. God will help you be the kind of mentor you need to be.

For some people, mentoring seems to come easy. Others find it more difficult and need more guidance and help. That's why this book was written. Pick and choose from these pages and use whatever helps you have a good relationship with the young person you are mentoring and to deal with issues that come up from time to time. Don't try to memorize it or to do everything that is suggested. Some things will work for you and some things won't. Compare the ideas you find here with your own experience and common sense. Adjust them to your own situation and needs. Above all, don't be afraid to enter your mentoring relationship not knowing what to do. That's part of the fun. Just be yourself.

There are few things more rewarding or exciting than walking with a young person across the bridge from childhood to adulthood. Some kids never make it, simply because there is no one there for them. We have a special opportunity to guide our young people not only into adulthood but into a vital relationship with Christ and the extended family of God—the church—one kid at a time.

On the next page is a Mentoring Covenant form that can be used to formalize the relationship you have with your young person. In the spaces provided, you and your young person can write in some of your intentions, goals, and expectations for the coming year.

Mentoring Covenant

between

_____

and

_____

For the twelve months beginning _____, we do hereby commit ourselves to walk together in friendship as a unique expression of our mutual desire to become faithful followers of Jesus Christ and responsible members of His church. We promise to help, support, encourage, and pray for each other, and, to the best of our abilities, participate in each others' lives in the following ways:

We will meet together on a regular basis.
Frequency:
Time:
Place:

We will try to accomplish the following goals:

We will try to do some of the following activities together:

Other understandings and provisions of this covenant:

Signed: _____
(mentor)

Signed: _____
(young person)

Date: _____

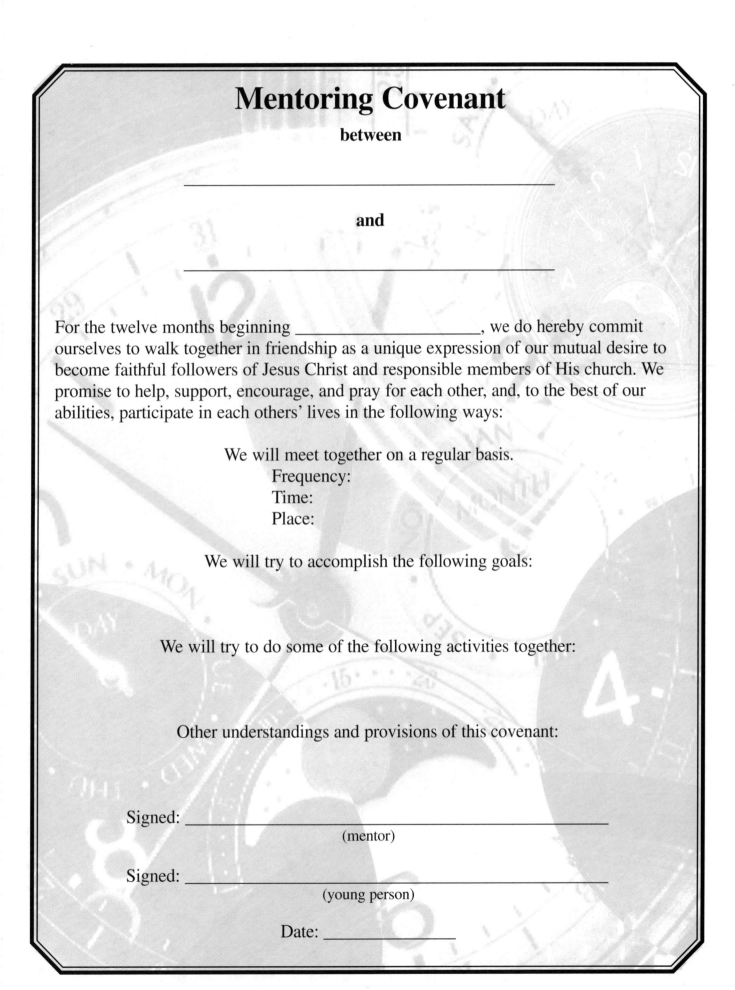

Mentoring Covenant

between

_____

and

_____

For the twelve months beginning _____, we do hereby commit ourselves to walk together in friendship as a unique expression of our mutual desire to become faithful followers of Jesus Christ and responsible members of His church. We promise to help, support, encourage, and pray for each other, and, to the best of our abilities, participate in each others' lives in the following ways:

We will meet together on a regular basis.
Frequency:
Time:
Place:

We will try to accomplish the following goals:

We will try to do some of the following activities together:

Other understandings and provisions of this covenant:

Signed: _____
(mentor)

Signed: _____
(young person)

Date: _____

Parent Affirmation

I do hereby affirm this mentoring relationship and give my son or daughter permission to participate in the activities that may result from it. In the event of illness or injury, I give my son or daughter's mentor permission to seek medical treatment as necessary should I not be reachable.

Signed: _____
(father)

Signed: _____
(mother)

Date: _____

Insurance company: _____

Policy number: _____

What Does a Mentor Do?

Chapter One

You're ready, willing, and anxious to get started. That's great, but what exactly do you do? There are no step-by-step instructions for mentoring. There are, however, some tips and suggestions that will help you be more effective as a mentor and prevent the kinds of serious mistakes that can ruin a mentoring relationship.

First Things First

To get your mentoring relationship off on the right foot, here are some things that should be done right away:

1. Make contact with the young person.

Once you are matched with a young person, let him or her know that you are really looking forward to being his or her mentor. Whether you know the young person or not, it's a good idea to send a card or letter, make a phone call, or meet at church or after school. Generate a little anticipation and excitement about the relationship by being positive and upbeat, perhaps suggesting some things that you might do together in the future.

2. Meet the young person's parents or guardians.

Before you begin meeting regularly with the young person, schedule a time when you can meet with the parents and the young person together. This would be a good time to tell the young person, in front of his or her parents, why you

17

want to mentor him or her. You can put people at ease if you share your desire to simply be an adult friend who cares and can offer help, encouragement, and support whenever needed. Let them know that you will be there to listen and that, except in rare circumstances, whatever the young person tells you will be kept in confidence. Explain that you are required to let parents or other authorities know when a young person is suicidal or involved in a behavior that is seriously self-destructive. Let them know that even in those circumstances you will act in the best interests of the young person. You will first encourage the young person to share with his or her parents what he or she has shared with you. Tell the parents that they should always feel free to call you if they have any questions or concerns.

Such a meeting will help both the parents and the young person better understand your role, and will put them both on equal footing. You don't want either of them to think that you can be played one against the other. A meeting like this will help get the relationship off to a good start and avoid potential problems that might come up later. Of course, it's a good idea to continue to make contact with the parents from time to time and to encourage them whenever you can.

3. Get acquainted with each other.

If you don't know your young person well, then it is important to take time to get acquainted. There are many activities that can be done with your young person simply to be together, to find out more about each other, and to build trust. Ideally, your relationship will be a long-term one, so there is no need to rush things.

4. Set up a regular meeting time and place.

In order for a good relationship to develop, you will need to be intentional about getting together regularly. This is the part of mentoring that requires some discipline. Set aside one day a week to meet. Offer several different options to your young person and agree on a time that is mutually acceptable to both of you. Kids can be incredibly busy, so try to be flexible. Try to allow enough time so that you are not rushed when you are together. The meeting place can vary, or it can be at the same place each time. You can meet at a local fast-food restaurant, a park, the church, or at home (yours or the young person's). The possibilities are endless, but the most important thing is to get it done. Don't be so flexible that it keeps getting put off.

5. Decide what you will do when you are together.

If you spend some time getting acquainted, you will probably discover some activities that you both enjoy. You may want to go fishing at a local lake, try cooking a meal together, shop at a thrift store, or help out at a rescue mission. You may want to work through some of the discussion activities that are provided in this book. Allow the young person to tell you the kinds of things he or she likes to do. Who knows, you just might enjoy playing laser tag or hanging out at the mall!

Seven Dos of Mentoring

After you have begun your mentoring relationship, it is important to keep it healthy and moving in the right direction. That's why it's important to keep the following dos and don'ts in mind.

Do be consistent.

All too often young people are let down by well-meaning adults who simply don't understand that "hope deferred makes the heart sick" (Proverbs 13:12). In the eyes of many young people, adults have a reputation of not being dependable. If we say that we will be there for our young person, but don't follow that up with our actions, then we send a message that the young person is not important. If your actions are consistent with your words, then you will increase the amount of trust between the two of you. You will build the young person's self image by giving him or her the message that he or she is really worth your time and effort. Satan will constantly cast doubt into the mind of your young person that the relationship will not last. Every time you are late for an appointment or cancel it, the young person may think that this is the beginning of the end of the relationship. Be a person of your word. Remember that "being there" is the most important aspect of mentoring.

Do be yourself.

There is absolutely no value in being anything but yourself. Trying to be someone else tells young people, who are very perceptive, several things. First, it says that you are insecure about your own identity. If you are confident with who you are, then you won't worry about what others think about you. Second, it sends a message to young people that you think you can fool them with phony behavior. Third, you will look like a fool! Remember that they are with you because of *who you are*, not because of *who you are not*. If you don't have confidence in who you are, how can you teach someone else to have confidence in who he or she is? You will never be as cool as their friends in the same way their friends are cool, but that doesn't mean they won't like or respect you.

Do learn to be a good listener.

If you want to be an effective mentor and friend, then learn to be a good listener. Being a good listener is not hard, but it takes practice and an understanding of the components of listening. Did you know that 55% of listening is visual? Or that 38% is determined by the tone of voice in your response and only 7% is verbal? In other words, when a person is determining whether you are listening or not, 55% of the information used to make that decision is based on what he or she sees you doing—your body language. When you respond, *the tone of your voice* will often carry more weight than the actual words you say. With that in mind, here are some helpful hints on how to be a better listener:

• *Maintain eye contact with the person you are listening to.* It is very distracting and discouraging to talk to someone who is looking around the room or daydreaming off into space.

• *Take notes on what he or she says.* That will help you remember later what the person said, and it sends a message that you are really paying attention.

• *Ask questions for clarification on anything you don't understand.* Ask questions to get more information and stay interested in what the person has to say.

• *Maintain a sympathetic and interested tone of voice.*

• *Avoid crossing your arms or leaning back in your chair as though you are not interested in what the person is saying.*

• *Avoid tapping your pencil or shaking your leg as though you can't wait for the person to stop talking so you can add your input.*

• *Don't interrupt or finish sentences for the person.* This is not only rude, but shows that you think your words are more important than his or hers.

• *Remember the acronym FAD.* It stands for *Focus, Accept,* and *Draw out.* First, focus on the person; give him or her your undivided attention. Second, show acceptance—with body language, leaning forward, acting interested. Then draw out—ask questions, encourage the person to tell you more. This will let the person know that you really do care about what he or she has to say.

Do be honest.

As a mentor, you are there to show kids that you love them and respect them. There is no love or respect in dishonesty. "Wounds from a friend can be trusted, but an enemy multiplies kisses" (Proverbs 27:6). It will be the truth that sets a young person free from the lies of the enemy, not patronizing dishonesty. Always tell the truth in love.

Do be patient and forgiving.

Kids will undoubtedly disappoint and hurt you. A mentor who wants to model the love of Jesus will hang in there and be forgiving. Forgiveness has been called "love without a net" because it is risky and takes us out of our comfort zones. That is how Jesus relates to us. He came as the suffering servant, and we must follow His example.

Keep in mind that when you are working with young people, you rarely get to see the results of what you are doing. That doesn't mean there won't be any. Results are sometimes not evident for ten or fifteen years, when the young person has grown and can look back and be grateful for all you did for him or her. The call to be a mentor is not a call to be successful, but to be faithful. So when you are getting frustrated, or it seems that things are not getting any better, hang in there and trust that God is doing some things through you that you just can't see. Practice patience.

Do encourage the young person you are mentoring.

Catch him or her in the act of doing something good. Praise him or her for saying the right thing. Thank him or her for doing a small thing right, even when he or she messes up a big thing. Be an encourager. Learn to affirm. If there is one characteristic you want to be known for, it is that of being a positive, encouraging person. Jesus was and is the ultimate encourager. He always has our best interests in mind. In Jeremiah 29:11, the Lord encourages us by saying that He has big plans "not to harm you, plans to give you hope and a future." In Psalm 139:17, 18, we read that God has us on His mind all of the time and that His thoughts are precious and as numerous as the sands of the sea. Jesus sees us in light of what we can become, not what we are. Remember that you represent this kind of friend—one who believes in people and believes that with God's help they can do anything Christ would want (Philippians 4:13). The sky's the limit.

Do pray daily for the young person you are mentoring.

We handicap ourselves when we try to save kids all by ourselves. God cares more about our young people than we do. If we are going to be effective as mentors, then we must pray daily that God will bless and multiply our efforts. Paul wrote to those he was mentoring: "Constantly I remember you in my prayers at all times" (Romans 1:9, 10). We also need to practice that kind of intercessory prayer.

Seven Don'ts of Mentoring

Don't play God.

Just because you are someone's mentor doesn't mean that his or her problems are now yours to solve. You are not a savior. You are not a problem solver so much as you are a source of wisdom and knowledge from which a young person can gain knowledge to solve his or her own problems. Wisdom is the proper use of knowledge. As you and your young person put your heads together, you can figure out how to use your collective knowledge to solve problems. Developing a process of problem solving will help your young person learn to work through life's difficulties. If you are constantly rescuing kids from their problems, eventually their problems will win because they won't know how to deal with them when you aren't there.

In the same way, you are not required to have an answer for everything. Don't try to give answers to every question. It would be better for you to admit that you don't know the answer than to give a wrong answer and look like a fool. When you are asked something you don't know, take that opportunity to teach the young person how to discover an answer for himself or herself.

Some people play God by acting as if they don't have any problems. They give the impression that they have it all together all of the time, or they act as though they always knew the things they know now. Kids need to know that you are human—not superhuman—and that you were once a lot like them. That gives them hope for the future. Be a Gabriel—a ministering angel sent to assist in time of need.

Don't compare the young person to yourself as a teenager, someone in your family, or another teenager.

This only breeds competition, resentment, and jealousy. Life is not a competition against the next person. We are to live as unto the Lord in the way He prescribes, regardless of what anyone else has done or is doing.

Sometimes we do this by projecting ourselves onto young people. We think they should behave as if they were us. It doesn't take kids long to figure out that you are living your life through them or that you are comparing them to yourself. Your goal is to help them become the people God created them to be, not a better version of yourself.

Don't lecture.

All day, young people are lectured to in school, at home, and at work. As a mentor, you can offer a listening ear more than a running mouth. Jesus never lectured someone into the kingdom; He loved them with a quiet and gentle spirit. Don't talk down to kids, nag, or yell at them. It is the power of truth that will set kids free (John 8:32). Rather than lecturing, help kids reflect, process their feelings, and learn from their experiences.

Don't let setbacks defeat you.

Every relationship has its ups and downs. Accept the fact that this one will too. Satan will work overtime to frustrate you and make you think it's time to throw in the towel. Remember that when you commit yourself to a relationship, your commitment has nothing to do with how you feel or whether the relationship is going well. It does, however, have everything to do with how you respond to adversity. If you are truly committed to the other person, then you will hang in there and keep trying despite the difficulties.

Don't judge or jump to conclusions.

The Bible says that "He who answers before listening—that is his folly and his shame" (Proverbs 18:13). There are usually at least two sides to every story. Kids like to tell stories about how unbearable and unfair things are at home, at school, or with friends. If you take them at face value you could get very protective and attempt to jump in and fix things. Things are rarely as bad or as good as they are described by an emotional kid. Before you jump to conclusions, give yourself time to investigate all of the facts. It's OK to give kids the benefit of the doubt, but don't choose sides or believe everything you hear. Check things out and try to find the truth. If you know what the truth is, then you will be in a better position to help your young person find solutions and make wise choices.

Don't play "Can You Top This?"

There have been instances when well-meaning adults have tried to impress young people with wild stories about their past. Sometimes it is tempting to exaggerate our own past to show kids how different we are today and how far we've come. While it is valuable to be honest and open with kids in certain circumstances, be sensitive not to glorify or make light of ungodly behavior that the young person may be struggling with and praying to be delivered from. I have heard mentors, youth workers, and other speakers talk to kids about their past experiences with illicit sex, illegal drugs, and criminal behavior as if they were proud of them. Use these stories carefully to glorify God, not your past.

Don't attempt to take the place of parents, pastors, teachers, or social workers.

It is vitally important to know your place and your boundaries in this relationship, especially in the beginning. Before a certain level of trust is developed, you are a friend who needs to be a good listener and encourager. As your relationship develops, you will sense how much your opinion is worth. In no way should you assume the responsibilities of already established authority figures—especially parents. You are there to support and supplement the efforts of these people, not subjugate them. Find out who the significant adults are in the life of your young person, and get to know them if you can. Remember, a relationship that is going to last takes time to develop. Don't jump to conclusions about how close you are or how much the young person likes or dislikes you. Take your time to develop a solid relationship through patience and trust.

Evaluating and Ending a Mentoring Relationship

One of the difficult parts of being a mentor is not knowing exactly how well you are doing. How do you know whether or not your efforts are paying off? How do you know if the young person is responding to you? How can you tell when it's time to end the relationship or allow the young person to get a new mentor? Evaluation is not always easy, but it's a good idea to take time now and then to reflect on the relationship and see if changes need to be made.

Chances are you didn't commit yourself to be a mentor to this particular young person forever. Usually, a twelve-month commitment is typical. It is a wonderful thing when you can recommit for another twelve months and keep the relationship going. How can you decide what to do? Here are some questions that can help you evaluate your mentoring relationship at the end of your term, or whenever you feel a need to evaluate.

• Are you and your young person comfortable with each other? Do you like each other and enjoy being together? If the answer is yes most of the time, then your mentoring relationship is in very good shape.
• Does your young person show up for meetings and activities that you have scheduled together? Do you? If so, then you are both doing great.
• On occasion, are you able to discuss sensitive issues with your young per-

son? Does he or she feel comfortable talking with you about personal issues, feelings, and problems? If so, this is the sign of a very strong relationship.

• Have you dealt with problems and conflicts in a positive way?

• If you filled out a covenant form at the beginning of the relationship, have you done what you originally committed yourselves to do?

• Have most (not all) of the meetings and activities you've done together been positive experiences?

Note that I haven't included questions such as: "Is your young person now going to church regularly, reading his or her Bible faithfully, and sharing Christ with his or her friends?" That's because such expectations are unrealistic and unfair—both to you and the young person. We can rejoice when kids do good things. However, we must be careful not to take the credit for their good behavior, nor to take the blame for their bad behavior. All we are called to do is to be faithful and to be there for our kids. We plant and cultivate, but God brings the harvest. We have been successful if young people just give us the opportunity to plant a few seeds along the way.

If you see some areas where you need to improve your relationship or change things, do it. Don't keep repeating the same mistakes over and over. Talk things over with your young person to find out how he or she feels about making some changes. Chances are the young person feels the same way you do.

Sometimes it is necessary to end the relationship or to change mentors. Your situation or the situation of your young person can change. Time commitments or other difficulties may make it impossible to meet regularly. Personalities may clash, and the relationship just might not click. As we mentioned earlier, every relationship has its ups and downs. You don't want to give up when things are in a down cycle. But if a relationship stays down for a long time and there doesn't seem to be much chance of it coming back up, it may be wise to end it and see if a new mentor can be found to take your place.

Ending a mentoring relationship can be painful for both parties. It shows a lot of maturity to be able to recognize when it's time to move on. It doesn't have to be regarded as a failure or a termination of a friendship. There are plenty of ways to remain friends. You may be able to remain a support mentor by praying and corresponding with the young person. Usually when there is pain, there is also something to rejoice about. When a person is experiencing physical pain, for example, it makes one thankful for good health. When a mentoring relationship has to end, it's a good time to be thankful for the successes that were experienced in the past and for what God is going to do in the future. ❧

Chapter Two

Understanding Adolescents

As a mentor to young people, it is important for you to have a basic understanding of the adolescent experience. Even though every adult has firsthand knowledge of adolescence, most adults have more or less "lost touch" with their adolescent years. It helps to be reminded of things that we once knew, and to learn why today's kids act and feel the way they do. In this section, I will summarize a few important developmental characteristics of young people and their families that will help you better understand the young person you are mentoring and why mentoring is so important.

Kids Are Still Kids

The first thing to remember is that today's kids have more in common with kids of the past than you may realize. It's true that kids today sometimes look different, talk a different language, and get involved in activities that are unique to this generation. But in most important ways, kids are the same. They are asking the same fundamental questions of identity and purpose that we all asked at their age: *Do you like me? Am I OK? What am I going to do? What am I going to be?* They struggle with how they look, how many friends they have, how their parents treat them, how to get through school, how to relate to the opposite sex, and all of those other things that drove us crazy when we were their age.

That's why it's important for mentors to try to remember their own adolescent years. The young people we are mentoring are feeling a lot of the same feelings that we once felt, and if we can remember what it was like, we'll be able to empathize and communicate a lot better.

A Different World

Why do kids today seem so different? Why do they behave in ways generations of the past never behaved? Why do they get into trouble so much? Why are so many kids put into institutions? Why do kids today need mentors?

There are no simple answers to questions like these, but one thing is very clear: today's kids are growing up in a very different world. All of us have been affected by the dramatic changes that have taken place in our society in recent years, but children and teenagers have been affected the most. The following are a few changes that have had a significant impact on kids.

1. Today's kids can no longer count on growing up in "normal" family situations.

Today, the abnormal is the normal. The divorce rate is over 50% and there are few kids who have the privilege of having a traditional two-parent family. Even those who have two parents rarely spend time with them because they are both working in order to keep up with today's expensive lifestyles. In addition, the extended family—a network of grandparents, uncles and aunts, and other relatives who live in the same geographic area—no longer exists for most young people. So today's kids grow up without the traditional support systems that existed for kids of the past.

Mentors have the opportunity to become part of a new kind of support system for today's kids. Even those who live in traditional family situations need other adults around them who will provide some support and guidance. Our job is to let kids know that they do have an extended family after all—the extended family of God.

2. Today's kids are no longer needed.

In the past, young people were viewed as assets. When they reached twelve or thirteen years of age, they were given responsibility for the family farm or the family business. In today's world, kids are liabilities, rather than assets. They have no place in the world where they can feel a sense of significance and purpose. This is why kids today are so vulnerable to self-destructive behavior. The suicide rate among teenagers has risen by 300% in the past twenty years. Like all human beings, young people have a great need to be needed, yet they realize very quickly that they are not. The need to be needed is greater than the need to be alive.

A mentor can help restore self-esteem and hope for kids who have come to believe that they have no inherent worth. God loves them for who they are, not what they do. We can model this in front of them by being friends and encouragers. In addition, we can help kids realize just how important they are to the kingdom of God. Nobody is "not needed" in God's kingdom. We can help our kids discover how to use their talents and abilities to change the world.

3. Today's kids are no longer protected from danger.

In the past, adults went out of their way to shield young people from anyone and anything that would harm them. That is no longer the case. Today's kids are exposed to everything that adults are exposed to. They watch a constant barrage of sex and violence on TV and at the movies. They learn how to use condoms before they learn how to read. Kids today have to learn to deal with potential child molesters, gun-toting classmates, and abusive parents. They must deal with more stress than any generation in history. It is no wonder that we talk about today's kids as being "at risk." There are few places they can go where they feel safe and out of harm's way.

The role of the mentor becomes clear when we think of all that kids are exposed to and are experiencing in today's world. They need a caring adult who will help them deal with the stress they are feeling and process the information that they are getting. The time that a young person spends with his or her mentor can become an oasis of safety in the middle of a hostile environment.

4. Today's kids are no longer given moral guidance and direction; instead, they are given choices.

Young people today have more choices available to them than ever before. They also have less guidance than ever before. No longer are moral choices a matter of right and wrong, good or bad, true or false. Everything today is a shade of gray; absolute truth has become a relic of the past.

Our young people face tough choices every day. Mentors have the opportunity to help young people learn how to make good choices. Kids need to be able to draw on the experience of adults in order to get a clear picture of what is true and what is false. The media doesn't worry about the truth. It worries only about what is entertaining, what gets the highest ratings, or what makes the most money. Kids want to know the truth, and we can be there to help them discover what it is.

Children Are Becoming Adults

Despite how the world has changed, there are some things that never change. Among them is the fact that children grow up and become adults. This change only happens to a person once in life, thank goodness, but it is a wonderful change nevertheless—much like a butterfly emerging from its cocoon.

Traditionally, the human life cycle looked something like this:

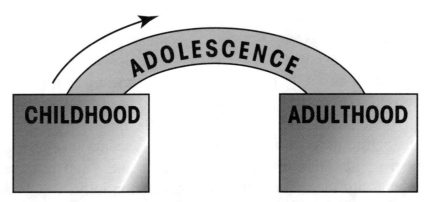

For thousands of years, adolescence was viewed as a relatively short transitional period in life when children became adults. As soon as a child reached puberty, cultures of the past celebrated this change of life with rites of passage. The tribe or community celebrated the fact that the child had become an adult and recognized the young person's new status. No longer was the young person considered a child; he or she instantly became an adult-in-training.

In those days, you knew exactly where you stood. In the Bible, for example, there are accounts of children and adults, but not "teenagers." That's because fourteen year olds in the ancient world were considered to be adults. That didn't mean they were necessarily mature and fully grown. It just meant that they were regarded as old enough to join the adult community and take their place alongside adults in apprenticeships and mentoring relationships. Mary, the mother of Jesus, was probably a young teenager when she gave birth to Jesus. To become a mother at that age was not unusual in ancient times.

In today's world, children are not regarded as young adults after puberty. They are regarded as teenagers, and teenagers do not have the rights and privileges of adults. Today, the human life cycle looks more like this diagram:

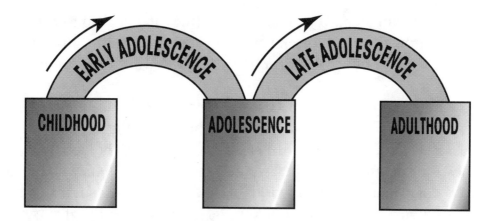

Here, adolescence is viewed as a separate stage of life. Adolescence is now a stage of life lasting ten or more years. Some people remain stuck in a kind of perpetual adolescence well into their twenties and thirties. One reason for this is that adolescence is a stage of life that excludes adults. Adolescence has its own culture and lifestyle, its own language and music. Adults look at it with disgust and assume that kids will eventually "grow out of it." But some never do; for them, adolescence is a dead-end street.

Adolescents need adults who will come alongside them during this stage of life and help them learn how to move on to the next stage—adulthood. Kids have a hard time learning how to become adults from other kids. They need to learn from adults who genuinely care about them and are willing to show them the way.

One way we can help teenagers make successful transitions to adulthood is to treat them like the young adults they are. They are not children. If we talk down to them all of the time and treat them like children, they will behave like children. If we treat them with dignity and respect and relate to them on a more mature level, their behavior will reflect that. When a group of teenagers is together with no adults present, they generally behave like a bunch of teenagers. If an adult is present, relating to the group on an adult-like level, the change in behavior is amazing to watch. Unfortunately, very few kids have adults around them who inspire them to higher levels of growth and development in their lives. That's why mentors are so special.

Kids Are Leaving the Nest

As children grow into adulthood, they become independent of their parents. A primary psychological task of adolescence is to find one's personal identity apart from parents. Young children are generally quite content to be under the watchful eye of their parents who make all the rules and decisions. As they get older (usually around age ten or eleven), however, they start thinking, *Hey, I want to make some of my own decisions and I don't want to be treated like a child anymore.*

This is all quite normal and necessary. Parents can't run their children's lives forever, and it is important for young people to develop responsibility for themselves. But in today's world, it is also dangerous. In the past, when kids "left the nest" to become adults, they were surrounded by adults who mentored them and accepted them into their world. In Luke 2, we find Jesus at age twelve leaving His parents and striking out on His own. Where do His frustrated parents find Him? He is surrounded by the elders in the temple, engaged in conversation and dialogue. Jesus found a group of adults outside His home who allowed Him the dignity of asking and answering questions. It's no wonder that "Jesus grew in wisdom and stature, and in favor with God and men" (Luke 2:52).

Today's kids leave the nest and, rather than finding adults to welcome them, simply hang out with other kids who are doing the same thing. The mentors' role is to be there as kids are trying to discover their own identities apart from their parents. Mentors can give teenagers important feedback and guidance that shapes their view of themselves and helps them grow into a healthy adulthood.

Adolescent Influences

Adolescents are easily influenced by their surroundings. As they become adults, a whole new world opens up to them and they want to take it all in. That's why they are easy targets for advertisers, the media, drug pushers, and promoters of the latest fads. Marketers spend billions of dollars each year trying to sell products to teenagers. They know that if they can sell a young person on their products, then he or she will be hooked for life.

Who do teenagers listen to most? Who has the greatest influence on them? Many people believe that kids are most influenced by their peers and the electronic media. That is not true. According to the best research we have, the primary influences on young people are as follows:

Parents
Other family members (grandparents, etc.)
Significant adults outside the home
Peer group (same age friends)
Media—TV, movies, music, etc.

Kids look first to parents for guidance and direction in life. Parents remain extremely influential during their children's adolescent years. Then comes the influence of other family members like grandparents, older brothers and sisters, uncles and aunts—assuming of course that these people are around. Next come significant adults, such as teachers, coaches, pastors, youth ministers, neighbors, parents of friends, and the like. The peer group and the media actually bring up the rear. That doesn't mean that the peer group and the media have no influence at all. They do have influence when it comes to things like popular clothing styles, leisure-time activities, music styles, etc. In terms of real influence—the kind that lasts a lifetime—their influence is not as great as some people imagine.

The problem today is that many kids have no parents who are there for them. Likewise, the extended family is nonexistent. Young people have no significant adults outside the home. The situation looks more like this:

~~Parents~~
~~Other family members (grandparents, etc.)~~
~~Significant adults outside the home~~
Peer group (same age friends)
Media—TV, movies, music, etc.

Take away the top three primary influences on young people, and the peer group and the media eventually rise to the top of the heap. It is true that for many kids today, the greatest influences on them are their peer group and the media. We must remember that *those things are only influential by default.* If parents, family members, and other adults were taking their rightful places, then the peer group and the media would be only minor influences.

Young people are very open to the influence of adults who care about them and are willing to be available for advice, encouragement, guidance, and wise counsel. Surveys have been done with the world's most successful people. The one thing they all have in common is *the influence of a significant adult* who had a powerful influence on them when they were young. As a mentor, you are in a privileged position to be that significant adult.

A Roller Coaster Ride

It is helpful to keep in mind that adolescents are in a transitional stage that affects every single aspect of their lives. Physically, the changes that take place are dramatic. Kids grow rapidly during adolescence and worry a great deal about how they are going to turn out. They will spend hours in front of mirrors trying to make themselves look good. It can become an obsession with some kids. As they get new bodies, they also begin to deal with their emerging sexuality. Many young people are sexually active today primarily because they have come to believe the lie that "everybody's doing it." They don't want to be left out. As mentors and friends, we can give kids the truth about sexuality and help them make decisions based on facts—not cultural myths.

Kids are also changing intellectually—how they think. When they were children, they thought in concrete terms. They accepted everything that came along as truth. But when children reach adolescence, they suddenly learn to think in a new way. They begin to challenge authority and question everything they previously accepted as truth. If things don't make sense to them, or if they seem unfair or wrong, kids will become argumentative and confrontational. A mentor can act as a sounding board for an inquisitive adolescent who is trying to figure out the world for himself or herself. We don't have to have all of the answers, but we can engage young people in dialogue and take their questions seriously.

Kids are changing emotionally as well. They will appear to undergo Dr. Jekyll and Mr. Hyde changes from one day to the next. One day you may have a young person who is your best friend, and the next day one who doesn't remember who you are. One day a young person will seem to be on fire for the Lord, and the next day he or she is doing drugs. Our tendency is to think that these kids are schizophrenic or at least hypocritical in their behavior. In reality, they are just trying to live on the emotional roller coaster that is adolescence. As they grow up, they begin to experience new emotions that can be very intense and unpredictable. The highs and lows can be extreme and result in some rather bizarre behavior. As kids learn to deal with their emotions, they try on different personalities to see which one fits them best. Young people will continue or cease various behaviors depending on the responses they get from family, friends, and other adults. We need to be patient with kids and give them the kind of positive feedback that will result in appropriate behavior.

The social changes of adolescence are equally significant. Little children need playmates, but adolescents need friends. Friends are people outside the home who offer the same kind of acceptance, love, and support that was previously provided by parents. For most kids today, the peer group or gang is their only source of friends. But kids also need and want adult friends. As a mentor, you can become that kind of friend—one who offers true friendship as a member of the body of Christ.

Spiritual Safety Net

Spiritually, young people are also changing. They are questioning the faith of their parents and the practices of their churches, all in an attempt to come up with a faith of their own. In most cases, they will end up with a faith that looks a lot like the faith of their parents (Proverbs 22:6). Meanwhile, kids sometimes act like they have no faith at all. Like the man on the flying trapeze, they are letting go of one trapeze to grab on to another, and while they are in flight, it looks pretty scary. If we are there as a safety net, pointing the way and encouraging kids to ask questions and discover the love of God, the power of Christ, and the faithfulness of the Holy Spirit for themselves, then they will eventually grab onto a trapeze of faith that will hold them and sustain them for the rest of their lives. Don't expect kids to be spiritually mature or to act like mature Christians while they are young. Be thankful for whatever progress you see, but don't put more of a burden on kids than they are able to bear. Be patient and forgiving and remember that the harvest is the Lord's, not ours. ❧

Fifty Things You and Your Kid Can Do Together

It is helpful to remember that the main ingredient in a mentoring relationship is your presence. You don't have to teach or counsel or do anything that sounds "mentor-like." Your primary goal in a mentoring relationship is to be a friend. Once the relationship is established, mentoring just "happens."

The following is a list of activities that may give you some ideas of things you and the young person you are mentoring can do together. Some of these activities are just for fun; others provide opportunities for instruction and learning. This list is not exhaustive, so add your own ideas to it.

1. Go to a ball game.

2. Have devotions.

3. Go bowling.

4. Work on a service project.

5. Go to a movie or rent a video. Discuss it afterward.

6. Go on a hike or cross-country skiing.

7. Ride bikes.

8. Go to the mall.

9. Help a homeless person.

10. Build a model airplane.

11. Play computer games.

12. Be a chauffeur for the young person and his or her date.

13. Wash a car—yours, the young person's, or even someone else's.

14. Visit a college.

15. Read through a book of the Bible. Try using Eugene Peterson's *The Message.*

16. Do the young person's chores.

17. Cook a meal.

18. Go fishing.

19. Fly a kite. Better yet, build your own kite and fly it.

20. Give the young person guitar lessons—or have him or her give you guitar lessons.

21. Attend a concert.

22. Play video games.

23. Go bungee jumping.

24. Play laser tag.

25. Work through a Bible study book.

26. Bake and decorate a birthday cake for someone.

27. Play a round of golf.

28. Go to an amusement park.

29. Go camping.

30. Chop wood.

31. Go hunting with a camera.

32. Fix a meal for a shut-in and deliver it.

33. Exercise—lift weights or do aerobics.

34. Play board games until two in the morning.

35. Make a quilt.

36. Go rock climbing.

37. Read a novel.

38. Visit a museum.

39. Look at old pictures.

40. Collect stamps.

41. Go swimming.

42. Secretly mow someone's lawn while the person is away.

43. Make a video.

44. Start a "Breakfast and Bible Study" group.

45. Make a snowman or go sledding.

46. Go for a walk on the beach or in the park.

47. Go to the airport and try to figure out where everybody is from.

48. Do homework.

49. Visit someone in the hospital.

50. Introduce the young person you are mentoring to your family. ❧

Chapter Four

Fifty Questions to Ask When Things Get Boring

There may be occasions when you get together with your young person and get stuck for something interesting or clever to say. After "Hi, how are you?" the conversation just dies and you sit there staring at each other. Well, don't worry if that happens. Sometimes silence is golden. But it might help if you take a couple of the following questions along with you—just in case. A single question can sometimes lead to all sorts of interesting dialogue. But you don't want to drop questions like bombs on the kid. Find a way to ask them in the context of whatever you are doing or to give a reason why a question is important or interesting to you. You don't want your young person to think that you are interrogating him or her. Remember—any question you ask of someone else, you should be willing to answer yourself.

1. What is your earliest memory?

2. If you could star in a movie, what would the movie be about?

3. If you could give your parents anything for Christmas, what would it be?

4. What gets you really depressed?

5. Have you ever broken a law?

6. What was your favorite TV show when you were eight years old?

7. If you could marry the perfect person, what would he or she be like?

8. If you could be a famous person, who would you like to be?

9. If you won the lottery, what would you do with the money?

10. What is your pet peeve?

11. What is the funniest joke you've ever heard?

12. What do you think your friends say about you when you're not around?

13. What do you think is the best age to get married?

14. What really makes you mad?

15. When was the first time you ever fell in love?

16. If you could plan your family's summer vacation, what would you do?

17. What do you think is the perfect age?

18. How would you like to be remembered after you die?

19. What is something that you are really proud of?

20. Is there one day in your life that you would like to live over?

21. If you had three wishes, what would they be?

22. Does crime pay?

23. How do you think Christians should be different from other people?

24. Is there a skill or hobby that you would like to learn?

25. What do you think of interracial marriages?

26. What is the best movie you've ever seen?

27. Have you ever had a recurring dream? If so, what is it?

28. What is the scariest thing that has ever happened to you?

29. What is your greatest fear?

30. If you could live anywhere, where would it be?

31. Where are your ancestors from?

32. What kinds of things do you like to read?

33. If you had the powers of Superman for one day, what would you do?

34. Who is God?

35. What do you think is hard about being a police officer?

36. If you could help someone become better at something, what would it be?

37. What part of the world would you like to visit?

38. Who is your favorite relative? Why?

39. Describe a perfect day.

40. If you could change one thing about yourself, what would it be?

41. If you could live at any time in history, when would it be?

42. What do you think happens after you die?

43. Do you think life should be "fair"? Has it been fair to you? Explain.

44. Do you think interracial dating is OK? Explain.

45. What is your favorite food?

46. If you could do anything in the world, what would you do?

47. What song do you think should get the award for number-one song of all time?

48. Who has been your best friend ever?

49. If you could be any animal in the world, which one would you be?

50. What do you think of TV evangelists? ❧

THE MENTORS IN MY LIFE

1. List several adults (excluding your parents) who had a positive influence on your life while you were a teenager. Under each name, describe the influence that person had on you.

      Name: _____
      Influence:

      Name: _____
      Influence:

      Name: _____
      Influence:

      Name: _____
      Influence:

      Name: _____
      Influence:

2. Why do you think these people were so influential to you?

3. Which of the qualities below do you think are important for adults who want to have a positive influence on today's youth? (Place a ★ next to each item that you think is extremely important; a ✔ next to each item that you think is important, but not necessary; and an ✘ next to any item that you don't think is either important or necessary.)

An effective mentor . . .

has patience.
is good-looking.
is compassionate.
has a sense of humor.
is mature.
is young.
loves God.
is honest.
is the same sex as the
   youth.
has money.
is cool.

is caring.
understands youth culture.
is courageous.
is unflappable.
knows Scripture.
has his or her own life
   together.
is forgiving.
has a lot of connections.
has time to give.
is intelligent.
loves kids.

is outgoing.
has high moral
   standards.
believes in prayer.
is a good
   communicator.
is athletic.
loves Jesus Christ.
has a strong family.
is respected by
   others.
likes rock music.

THE SEVEN DOS OF MENTORING

Instructions: Read each of the statements below and check those that you are willing to commit yourself to. If you check all seven, sign your name at the bottom and keep this list handy as a constant reminder of what good mentoring is all about.

❏ BE CONSISTENT
I will be dependable and trustworthy as a mentor. To the best of my ability, I will honor my commitments and keep my promises. I *will be there* for the youth I am mentoring on a regular and consistent basis for as long as I am required to do so.

❏ BE YOURSELF
I will be thankful for who I am—for the personality, gifts, talents, abilities, and attributes that God has specifically given to me. I believe that God knows me, loves me, and has called me to serve as a mentor to youth. And I am confident that He will be able to use me just the way I am.

❏ BE A LISTENER
I will take every opportunity to be a good listener in my mentoring relationship. I will avoid judging and lecturing. I will listen attentively because I care, and because I desire to treat the youth I am mentoring with dignity and respect.

❏ BE HONEST
I will do my best to tell the truth always in my mentoring relationship, even when it hurts. In so doing, I will inspire the youth I am mentoring to be honest with me. When either of us is unsure of the truth, we will be honest with each other and seek to discover the truth together.

❏ BE PATIENT AND FORGIVING
I will be realistic about the expectations I have for the youth I am mentoring. I will do my best to demonstrate unconditional love in every circumstance by being gracious, understanding, slow to anger, patient, and forgiving. I will not allow failures to destroy our relationship.

❏ BE ENCOURAGING
I will bring out the best in the youth I am mentoring by being generous with affirmation, encouragement, gratitude, and praise. I will do all that I can to inspire my youth to dream dreams and to recognize the potential that he or she has in Christ Jesus.

❏ PRAY HARD
I will not become frustrated or discouraged because of my inability to change a young person's life. Instead, I will pray daily for the youth I am mentoring, and trust God to do what I cannot do.

Signed _____

THE SEVEN DOS OF MENTORING

Instructions: Read each of the statements below and check those that you are willing to commit yourself to. If you check all seven, sign your name at the bottom and keep this list handy as a constant reminder of what good mentoring is all about.

❏ BE CONSISTENT

I will be dependable and trustworthy as a mentor. To the best of my ability, I will honor my commitments and keep my promises. I *will be there* for the youth I am mentoring on a regular and consistent basis for as long as I am required to do so.

❏ BE YOURSELF

I will be thankful for who I am—for the personality, gifts, talents, abilities, and attributes that God has specifically given to me. I believe that God knows me, loves me, and has called me to serve as a mentor to youth. And I am confident that He will be able to use me just the way I am.

❏ BE A LISTENER

I will take every opportunity to be a good listener in my mentoring relationship. I will avoid judging and lecturing. I will listen attentively because I care, and because I desire to treat the youth I am mentoring with dignity and respect.

❏ BE HONEST

I will do my best to tell the truth always in my mentoring relationship, even when it hurts. In so doing, I will inspire the youth I am mentoring to be honest with me. When either of us is unsure of the truth, we will be honest with each other and seek to discover the truth together.

❏ BE PATIENT AND FORGIVING

I will be realistic about the expectations I have for the youth I am mentoring. I will do my best to demonstrate unconditional love in every circumstance by being gracious, understanding, slow to anger, patient, and forgiving. I will not allow failures to destroy our relationship.

❏ BE ENCOURAGING

I will bring out the best in the youth I am mentoring by being generous with affirmation, encouragement, gratitude, and praise. I will do all that I can to inspire my youth to dream dreams and to recognize the potential that he or she has in Christ Jesus.

❏ PRAY HARD

I will not become frustrated or discouraged because of my inability to change a young person's life. Instead, I will pray daily for the youth I am mentoring, and trust God to do what I cannot do.

Signed _____

How to Use Talk Starters

During your mentoring relationship, you will want to take time to talk with your youth about a variety of important topics. This will give you the chance to find out what your youth believes and will also give you a chance to share what you believe. Many times these conversations will happen naturally as the result of normal interaction and experiences you have together. But there will be other times when you will need a way to create interest or generate dialogue on the topic that you want to discuss. That's what Talk Starters are for. They can be used to help stimulate good discussion on a variety of topics.

Here is how to use them:

1 Use them sparingly. Don't pull out Talk Starters every time you get together with your youth. They will become rather dull and boring very quickly. But if they are used on an occasional basis, or whenever the youth seems open to discuss a particular topic, they can be very helpful. For example, if your youth brings up questions about the importance of going to church, you might suggest doing the "Church" Talk Starter together. If you notice that your youth is having a difficult time with her anger, there is a Talk Starter on the subject of anger that might be very helpful. Use Talk Starters sparingly and wisely.

2 If you know which Talk Starter you want to use with your youth ahead of time, make two photocopies of it and bring it to your meeting. Don't bring the Mentor Handbook.

3 Go through the Talk Starter ahead of time yourself to acquaint yourself with it and to prepare in advance some possible responses that you might need during your discussion. Look up the Scripture verses and familiarize yourself with them before you meet.

4 Have a Bible handy. You will also need a pen or pencil for both of you.

5 Don't do the Talk Starter in a place that is noisy, or where there are too many distractions. It's not usually a good idea to try to work through a Talk Starter at a busy McDonald's, for instance. It would be best to go to a park, or to the library, or to some other place where there is relative peace and quiet.

6 When you are ready to do the Talk Starter, let your youth know that you are genuinely interested in what he or she thinks about that particular topic. The Talk Starter will help accomplish this. Don't make it sound like you are going to do a Bible lesson together. Ask him or her to answer the questions on the sheet, and explain that you will do the same. Then you can compare answers with each other.

7 Take time to answer the questions. You can take them one at a time (with discussion in between), or you can do them all at once.

8 Make sure that your youth understands that there are no "correct" answers to these questions. There is no answer quide. You want him or her to write down exactly how he or she feels, or what he or she believes is true. He or she should not try to answer the question in order to please you or anyone else. He or she should not try to guess what the "Christian" response would be. He or she is simply to be honest. You will do the same on yours.

9 The discussion may simply focus on your responses to each question. Ask the youth to share his or her answers with you, and then you can share yours with him or her. Along the way, you will have the opportunity to hear what he or she is thinking on the subject, and you will have a chance to share your views as well. Most of the Talk Starters offer some additional help on the subject—in the introduction or in sidebars.

10 Remember that this is a good time to practice your listening skills. (Remember FAD.) Don't monopolize the discussion. Allow your youth to share his or her thoughts with you without interruption. Ask a lot of questions. Find out more information. Affirm the answers that are given. If you don't agree with him or her, don't put him or her down or criticize. Let your youth know that you are thankful that he or she is so open and honest with you.

11 Don't feel like you have to finish all of the questions on the sheet. You may get a lot of discussion out of just one of the questions. That's fine. Skip those that don't seem as important for you to spend time on. You may want to use one Talk Starter for several weeks. Some of them will generate hours of discussion.

12 Each Talk Starter concludes with "God's Perspective." Use this activity to share some insights from the Bible. Avoid preaching here, but allow the Scripture passage to speak for itself. If you can add some insights, feel free to do so, but allow the youth to think about the Scripture passage himself or herself and to share his or her thoughts on what the passage might be saying on the subject.

13 The optional activities that are listed are for your use if you wish to continue learning more about this subject with your youth. In some cases, this is an important thing to do. You will be able to tell which subjects are of great interest to your youth, and you really should follow up with additional discussion and learning on the subject. The optional activities are only suggestions. You may be able to think of other ways to apply the material together.

14 Pray for wisdom and guidance from God when you use Talk Starters. You will notice that there are no answer guides, no "leader's material" to help you teach from them. They are simply tools to be used to stimulate conversation. You will have to make your own decisions about which direction your conversation should go. You will hear things that you will need real wisdom and self-control in responding to. You may hear things that are private, sensitive, or even dangerous. How will you respond? What will you do with information that shocks you or makes you angry? You can prepare for situations such as these by asking God to be with you and to help you be understanding, compassionate, and wise.

SETTING GOALS

"Where there is no vision, the people perish"
(Proverbs 29:18, KJV).

If you don't know where you're going, you'll never get there. Lack of direction nearly always results in confusion and hopelessness. Everyone wants to succeed, but if a person never takes the time to decide on a specific path to success, he or she will never achieve it.

An airline pilot came on the intercom during a long flight and announced to the passengers, "I've got some good news and some bad news. The good news is we're making good time. The bad news is we're lost." Many people are busy today—engaged in all kinds of activity—but they are lost. They are like the people in that airplane—going nowhere fast.

A goal is like a destination, a target. If you don't have a target, you aren't going to hit anything—or, you may hit something that you didn't want to hit. To be successful in life, you need to set some goals for success. Very few people became successful in life by *accident, luck,* or *chance.*

WISHES, HOPES, AND GOALS
Do you know the difference between a wish, a hope, and a goal?

A **wish** identifies your *desire.* ("I wish I could play on the basketball team.") Complete the following sentences:
• I wish I were . . .

• I wish I could . . .

• I wish I had . . .

A **hope** identifies your *dream.* ("I hope the coach chooses me to be on the team.") Complete the following sentences:
• I hope I am . . .

• I hope I can . . .

• I hope I have . . .

A **goal** identifies your *intention* or *commitment* to achieve your desires and dreams. ("My goal is to make the basketball team.") Complete the following sentences:

• My goal is to . . .

• My goal is to . . .

• My goal is to . . .

HOW TO REACH A GOAL
It is sometimes helpful to remember the five D's of reaching goals:
1. *Detail:* Make a list of the steps necessary to reach your goal.
2. *Detour:* Expect obstacles along the way and go around them.
3. *Decide:* Choose a plan of action. Decide on a time line.
4. *Determine:* Commit yourself to follow through. Don't give up.
5. *Do:* Go for it! Start reaching your goal.

HERE ARE EXAMPLES OF SOME POSSIBLE GOALS:
• To decide on a career
• To find a job
• To get a college degree
• To learn how to ice skate
• To learn how to operate a computer
• To paint my bedroom
• To buy a new coat
• To help someone less fortunate than me
• To lose five pounds
• To apologize to someone I hurt

DETAIL
Big goals can often be broken down into smaller goals. These smaller goals are the steps you take to reach the big goal. For example, if your goal is to get a high school

diploma, the following smaller goals must be accomplished:

1. Get up every morning on time.
2. Go to class every day.
3. Do all of the homework.
4. Graduate!

Think about one of the goals you wrote earlier. What smaller goals (steps) will enable you to reach your goal?

DETOUR

What are some of the obstacles that might prevent you from reaching your goal?

How might you overcome these obstacles?

What will you do if you fail? Choose the best answer.

_____ I'll probably give up.
_____ I'll change my goal.
_____ I'll make some adjustments and try again.
_____ I won't fail.
_____ I don't know what I'll do.

DECIDE

When you would like to reach your goal? Choose the best answer.

_____ One week from now
_____ One month from now
_____ Three months from now
_____ Six months from now
_____ One year from now
_____ Three years from now
_____ Five years from now
_____ Other: _____

What is the first thing you plan to do toward reaching your goal?

When can you complete this first step?

_____ Today or tomorrow
_____ This week
_____ This month
_____ Within three months
_____ Within the next year
_____ Other: _____

DETERMINE

Can you commit yourself to reaching your goal now?

Is there someone who can help you reach your goal? If so, who?

DO

The only thing left now is to get started. Now that you have identified your goal and know what it will take to reach it, your chances for success are good.

It would be a good idea to evaluate how you are doing from time to time. Pick a date now for your first evaluation.

OPTIONAL ACTIVITIES

• Go to the public library to look up information on your goal. Visit other places where information might be available. For example, if your goal is to become a radio announcer, visit a radio station to see if you can get a tour or talk to someone who can give you information.

• Interview someone who has achieved the same goal or a person who has become successful in another field. Find out how that person was able to reach his or her goal. Get some advice from him or her.

A GOAL MUST BE:

• _Yours._ It can't be your parents' goal or your friend's goal or your mentor's goal. It has to be _your_ goal—one that you really want to achieve.
• _Clear._ Some goals are so vague that they are impossible to reach. You need to be able to know when you've achieved that goal. For example, "My goal is to be happy" is not really a goal. It's a nice thought, but it isn't a goal. Instead, you need to identify goals that will make you happy like "My goal is to get an A or B on the history final next month."
• _Realistic._ Your goal must be attainable. That doesn't mean you can't shoot high. Just make sure that you understand what's involved and are prepared to do what's necessary to reach that goal. It needs to be within the range of your ability. If you are only five feet tall, it is probably not a good idea to plan on a career in the NBA—at least not until you grow another eighteen inches.
• _Under your control._ Reaching your goal should be up to you, not someone else. For example, you shouldn't have "to win the lottery" as a goal. You have no control over that. You could have "to save $1,000 for a down payment on a car" as a goal, because that is something you have control over. You can earn and save the money so that you will eventually have $1,000.

FAMILY

"Be completely humble and gentle; be patient, bearing with one another in love" (Ephesians 4:2).

When my children were young, we moved into a new neighborhood. The kids living there already knew each other, and my children—being the new kids on the block—wanted to play with them.

The first day seemed fine. They met the other kids and played fine, but the next week, things changed. The kids rode past my kids and said, "We aren't playing today," and proceeded to go about their business. This went on for about five days and my kids began to wonder what they did to make the other kids not want to play with them anymore. I asked my daughters if it bothered them and one said, "A little." My youngest daughter, however, said, "No, because I have my brother and sister to play with."

It made me feel good that my daughter considered her family to be a place of safety and refuge from the world. That's the way it should be. God created us to be in families. No one was meant to be alone in the world.

Families are very important and wonderful to be a part of, but they can also be a source of pain and stress. There are very few families that are free from problems.

There are countless definitions for a family today. Some would say a family is "a group of people who are related to each other in some way" or "a group of people who live together in the same house" or "a mother and a father and their children." How would you describe your family?

Think of some famous TV families. Which one do you like best? Why?

Would you like your family to be like this family? Explain.

Think of your own family. List three things you like about your family.
1.
2.
3.

List three things that you don't like about your family.
1.
2.
3.

If you could change one thing about your family, what would it be?

In a family, people play different roles. What roles do you play in your family?
(a) The Troublemaker
(b) The Breadwinner
(c) The Loud Mouth
(d) The Slave
(e) The Comedian
(f) The Peacemaker
(g) The Cheerleader
(h) The Black Sheep
(i) The Invisible Man or Woman
(j) The _____

Rate your family from 1 (seldom) to 5 (often) in the following areas:

- My family spends a lot of time together.
  1   2   3   4   5

- Members of my family care a lot about each other.
  1   2   3   4   5

- My family has a lot of fun when we are together.
  1   2   3   4   5

- When a problem comes up, my family is able to solve it.
  1   2   3   4   5

- There is good communication in my family.
  1   2   3   4   5

- My family does its best to be a good Christian family.
  1   2   3   4   5

- There is a lot of laughter in my family.
  1   2   3   4   5

List three things you could do to help improve your family life.

1.

2.

3.

GOD'S PERSPECTIVE

Look up the following Scripture passages. See if you can apply or relate them to *your* family.

- Proverbs 6:20-22

- Ephesians 6:1-4

- Romans 12:9-12

OPTIONAL ACTIVITY

- Why not write a letter to your parents—or to a brother or sister—letting them know that you love them and care about them? If you find it hard to write a letter like that, then simply offer some words of encouragement and support.

SELF-IMAGE

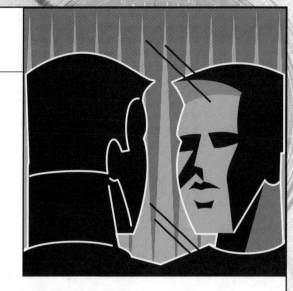

"I am fearfully and wonderfully made" (Psalm 139:14).

Moses was a man in the Bible who was challenged by God to do something very important. God asked Moses to confront the leader of Egypt and demand that he set free the 2,000,000 Jews who were held as slaves.

But Moses was scared. He gave God all kinds of excuses as to why he couldn't do it. He said he couldn't talk. He said he wasn't very smart. He said there were other people who were better qualified. Finally, he just said, "No!" (See Exodus 3–4.)

Moses kept focusing on all of his shortcomings and faults, and it immobilized him. His self-image problem kept him from being used by God. But God's response was simple and direct. God said, in effect, "You're right, Moses. You do have shortcomings, but they don't matter. I made you exactly the way I want you to be. And I gave you all of the abilities you need. So go, Moses, and remember that *I will be with you* at all times."

In other words, God told Moses, "*Who* you are is not as important as *whose* you are." All of us have faults, weaknesses, and shortcomings. We all have plenty of excuses for not doing what God wants us to do. We don't have the right family, the right appearance, the right abilities, or the right financial situation. But God's response is just like the response He gave to Moses: "I made you and you are Mine. You are My beloved child and I will *always* be with you."

The world keeps telling us that we don't have what it takes. If we keep listening to that voice, we will always have a lousy self-image. But there is another voice, the voice of God, telling us the truth about who we are. It is God's voice we must listen to.

When I look in the mirror, I . . . (check all that apply to you)
____ feel pretty good about myself.
____ hate the way I look.
____ wish I were somebody else.
____ smile.
____ get depressed.
____ see a person with a lot of problems.
____ feel proud to be the person I am.
____ feel confident and self-assured.
____ don't like this person.
____ wish I had a new body.
____ don't think about my looks too much.
____ see a person who was created in the image of God.
____ worry that nobody will like me.
____ other: _____

Put an "X" on the lines below at the point that best indicates how you feel about yourself.

1	2	3	4	5
A loser				A winner

1	2	3	4	5
Stupid				Intelligent

1	2	3	4	5
Unattractive				Good-looking

1	2	3	4	5
Incompetent				Capable

1	2	3	4	5
An unlikable person				A likable person

THOUGHT TO REMEMBER
"If you want to be respected by others, the first step is to have a proper respect for yourself."
—Dostoevsky

BORN TO FLY

One day a prairie chicken found an egg and sat on it until it hatched. Unbeknownst to the prairie chicken, the egg wasn't a prairie chicken egg; it was an eagle egg. For some reason, the egg had been abandoned, so an eagle was born into a family of prairie chickens.

While the eagle is the greatest of all birds, soaring above the heights with grace and ease, the prairie chicken doesn't even know how to fly. In fact, prairie chickens are so lowly that they eat garbage.

Predictably, the little eagle, being raised in a family of prairie chickens thought he was indeed a prairie chicken. He walked around, ate garbage, and clucked like a prairie chicken.

Then one day, he looked up and saw a majestic eagle soar through the air, dipping and turning. He asked what it was and his family said, "It's an eagle. But you could never be like that because you are just a prairie chicken." The eagle spent his whole life looking up at eagles, longing to join them among the clouds. But it never once occurred to him to lift his wings and try to fly himself. The eagle died thinking he was just a prairie chicken.

—From *Hot Illustrations for Youth Talks* by Wayne Rice (Zondervan/Youth Specialties)

Make a list of some of your good qualities.
1.
2.
3.
4.
5.

Make a list of some of your not-so-good qualities.
1.
2.
3.
4.
5.

(Now put an "X" beside the ones you think you can improve.)

Check the following sentences that reflect how you think about yourself.

That's Me	That's Not Me	
____	____	I'm good enough, I'm smart enough, and doggone it, people like me.
____	____	I think I am better than most people.
____	____	I don't take criticism very well.
____	____	I'll do almost anything to have friends.
____	____	Other people seem to have it easier than I do.
____	____	I put myself down too much.
____	____	I feel confident about myself most of the time.
____	____	I'm proud of who I am.
____	____	I always worry that people won't like me.
____	____	I know that God loves me just the way I am.

In terms of self-image, what matters most to you? Rank the following items from most important (1) to least important (12).

____ How I look
____ How much money I have
____ My accomplishments
____ What God thinks of me
____ What my family thinks of me
____ What other people think of me
____ My background
____ How I dress
____ My character
____ My job
____ My intelligence
____ My influence on others

GOD'S PERSPECTIVE

Read the following Scripture passages. See what they have to say about your self-image.

• Genesis 1:26-27

• I Samuel 16:7

• Psalm 8:4-8

• Psalm 139:13-18

• Psalm 147:10, 11

• John 3:16

OPTIONAL ACTIVITIES

• Keep a daily journal for at least a month. Every day, write down how you feel about yourself.

• One of the best ways to get rid of a low self-image is to stop thinking about yourself so much and help other people. Take time to affirm others and to find ways to serve others during the next few weeks.

FRIENDS

"There is a friend who sticks closer than a brother"
(Proverbs 18:24).

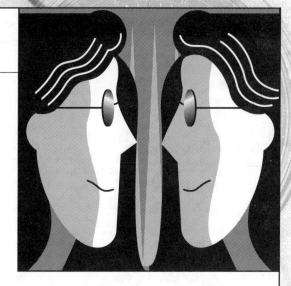

Everybody wants to have friends. You can get pretty lonely without friends. According to the dictionary, a friend is "a person you know well who is on your side; someone who is supportive, helpful and reliable." Little kids want playmates, but young people and adults want friends. A friend is someone you want to be with because he or she likes you and cares about you—and vice-versa.

Make a list of ten people you know. Choose from the following categories: friends from school, friends from church, friends in your neighborhood, adult friends, a boyfriend or girlfriend, friends who live out of town, and family members.

1.

2.

3.

4.

5.

6.

7.

8.

9.

10.

Mark your friends with a symbol according to the following chart:

◆ = A very close friend; we are almost inseparable.

✳ = A good friend; we spend time together and have fun together.

■ = A casual friend; we don't spend much time together.

Who is your very best friend right now?

What makes this person such a good friend? What do you like most about him or her?

Check the following statements that you agree with.

_____ I would like to have more friends.

_____ My friends have a good influence on me.

_____ I have a difficult time making friends.

_____ I'd like to trade in some of my friends for new ones.

_____ My parents don't like my friends.

_____ I choose the right kind of friends.

_____ Most of my friends are Christians.

_____ I get along with my friends.

_____ Some of my friends have hurt me.

Which of the following characteristics of a friend are most important to you? Rank them from 1 (most important) to 10 (least important).

_____ Same age as me

_____ Likes to do the same things that I like

_____ Popular

_____ Christian

_____ Lives close to me

_____ High moral standards

_____ Has no other friends

_____ Comes from a good family

_____ Has money

_____ Trustworthy

What do you think you should do if some of your friends are getting you into trouble or having a negative influence on you?

GOD'S PERSPECTIVE

Read the following Scripture passages. See what they have to say about friendships.

- Job 2:11

- Ecclesiastes 4:10

- I Corinthians 15:33

- II Corinthians 6:14

OPTIONAL ACTIVITY

• Interview your parents or some other adults. Ask them to answer the following questions (or any others you want to ask) about friends.

1. Who was your best friend when you were my age?

2. What do you remember most about that friend?

3. Is that person still your friend? Do you stay in touch now? Why or why not?

QUALITIES OF FRIENDSHIP

In the Bible, the following eight characteristics of friendship are found in Colossians 3:12-14.

1. *Compassion* (I try to see things from my friends' points of view.)
2. *Kindness* (I take every opportunity to do nice things for my friends.)
3. *Humility* (I try to build up and encourage my friends.)
4. *Gentleness* (I treat my friends as I want to be treated. I avoid hurting them.)
5. *Patience* (I am willing to go the extra mile with my friends.)
6. *Support* (I try to help my friends whenever they need me.)
7. *Forgiveness* (I forgive my friends, rather than hold a grudge or try to get even.)
8. *Love* (I let my friends know that I really care about them.)

FRIENDS

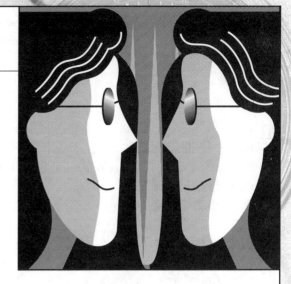

"There is a friend who sticks closer than a brother"
(Proverbs 18:24).

Everybody wants to have friends. You can get pretty lonely without friends. According to the dictionary, a friend is "a person you know well who is on your side; someone who is supportive, helpful and reliable." Little kids want playmates, but young people and adults want friends. A friend is someone you want to be with because he or she likes you and cares about you—and vice-versa.

Make a list of ten people you know. Choose from the following categories: friends from school, friends from church, friends in your neighborhood, adult friends, a boyfriend or girlfriend, friends who live out of town, and family members.

1.

2.

3.

4.

5.

6.

7.

8.

9.

10.

Mark your friends with a symbol according to the following chart:

◆ = A very close friend; we are almost inseparable.

✳ = A good friend; we spend time together and have fun together.

■ = A casual friend; we don't spend much time together.

Who is your very best friend right now?

What makes this person such a good friend? What do you like most about him or her?

Check the following statements that you agree with.

____ I would like to have more friends.

____ My friends have a good influence on me.

____ I have a difficult time making friends.

____ I'd like to trade in some of my friends for new ones.

____ My parents don't like my friends.

____ I choose the right kind of friends.

____ Most of my friends are Christians.

____ I get along with my friends.

____ Some of my friends have hurt me.

Which of the following characteristics of a friend are most important to you? Rank them from 1 (most important) to 10 (least important).

____ Same age as me

____ Likes to do the same things that I like

____ Popular

____ Christian

____ Lives close to me

____ High moral standards

____ Has no other friends

____ Comes from a good family

____ Has money

____ Trustworthy

What do you think you should do if some of your friends are getting you into trouble or having a negative influence on you?

GOD'S PERSPECTIVE

Read the following Scripture passages. See what they have to say about friendships.

- Job 2:11

- Ecclesiastes 4:10

- I Corinthians 15:33

- II Corinthians 6:14

OPTIONAL ACTIVITY

- Interview your parents or some other adults. Ask them to answer the following questions (or any others you want to ask) about friends.

1. Who was your best friend when you were my age?

2. What do you remember most about that friend?

3. Is that person still your friend? Do you stay in touch now? Why or why not?

QUALITIES OF FRIENDSHIP

In the Bible, the following eight characteristics of friendship are found in Colossians 3:12-14.
1. *Compassion* (I try to see things from my friends' points of view.)
2. *Kindness* (I take every opportunity to do nice things for my friends.)
3. *Humility* (I try to build up and encourage my friends.)
4. *Gentleness* (I treat my friends as I want to be treated. I avoid hurting them.)
5. *Patience* (I am willing to go the extra mile with my friends.)
6. *Support* (I try to help my friends whenever they need me.)
7. *Forgiveness* (I forgive my friends, rather than hold a grudge or try to get even.)
8. *Love* (I let my friends know that I really care about them.)

EDUCATION

"Study to show yourself approved" (II Timothy 2:15, NKJV).

When you are in school, sitting in class and bored to death, you may sometimes wonder, *What's the point? How am I ever going to use this stuff in real life? What possible connection does world history or algebra have with anything that is important to me?*

When I was playing defensive back in the NFL, a lot of people asked me if we just got in the huddle and said, "Go get 'em, cover your guy, let's go!" Nothing could be further from the truth. Even though I played defense, we had over fifty plays per game. Each play had about five different variations, all of which could be called in one play. We would make our call in the huddle; then, after we lined up and saw what the offense was doing, we could change that play as many as three times.

On top of that, we not only had to understand all of our defensive plays, but we had to learn all of the offensive plays of the opposing team. Each week, we spent more time in the classroom than on the practice field. We had written exams almost every day and a nine-page exam the day before each game. We had to know all of *our* plays, all of *their* plays, and what to do in every situation.

My point is this—if you think you don't need an education to succeed in life, think again. Football players who don't take getting an education seriously usually don't make it because they don't know how to study and learn. The same is true for every other career. Education is important; it will unlock the future for you.

Dream a little bit. If you could be or do anything in the world, what would you be?

If you quit school today, what would you do with your life? List some of the jobs that you could get.

1.

2.

3.

Think about the "dream life" you just described. What kind of an education would you need to do this? What subjects in school are most important in this field?

Do you agree or disagree with the following statements?

A   D   School is basically a waste of time.

A   D   The only reason you need school is to be able to get a good job and make a lot of money.

A   D   If you are a successful student, you'll probably be a successful person.

A   D   I could do better in school if the teachers were better.

A   D   I enjoy learning new things.

A   D   I could probably get better grades if I tried harder.

A   D   School causes a lot of stress in my life.

A   D   People who study a lot and get good grades don't have a social life.

A   D   Most of my friends are good students.

Complete the following sentences by writing in a letter grade (A, B, C, D, or F).

1. My grade average in school right now is approximately a(n) ____.

2. If I applied myself and worked hard, my grade point average would probably be a(n) ____.
3. In my favorite subject at school, I usually get a(n) ____.
4. In my least favorite subject at school, I usually get a(n) ____.
5. If I could give my school a grade, I'd give it a(n) ____.
6. Overall, the teachers at my school should get a grade of ____.

JIMMY AND THE GENIE

Once upon a time there was a boy named Jimmy who was walking in the desert when he found a magic lantern on a pile of rocks. Jimmy thought, *Maybe if I rub this lantern, a genie will come out and grant me three wishes!* He tried it, and sure enough, a genie appeared. Jimmy was very excited and asked the genie for three wishes. But the genie replied, "I'm not that kind of genie. I give advice."

"Oh," said Jimmy, "then give me some advice."

"Pick up as many rocks as you can and take them home with you," said the genie, just before he disappeared.

"This is stupid," said Jimmy. "I have a long way to go and these rocks are heavy. I'm not going to pick up any rocks!" He did pick up one rock, however, and stuck it in his pocket.

When he finally got home, Jimmy took off his dirty clothes to be washed. His mother went through his pockets and found the rock. She asked Jimmy where he got the rock. Jimmy replied, "Oh, some stupid genie told me to pick up a bunch of them, but I only picked up one."

"Jimmy!" his mother cried. "This isn't a rock. This is the biggest diamond I've ever seen."

Unfortunately, Jimmy was never able to find that pile of rocks again.

Moral: *What seems useless to us today may become a diamond tomorrow.*

What is your favorite class at school? Why?

Who is your favorite teacher? Why?

Which of the following things do you think would help you get better grades in your least favorite classes?
____ Get some tutoring
____ Change my study habits
____ Take better notes in class
____ Change schools
____ Cheat
____ Talk to my teacher about getting some additional help
____ Go to the library more
____ Find some friends who are good students
____ Stop cutting class
____ Get more sleep at night
____ Learn to use a computer

Is there any reason why you can't do any of the items that you've checked? If so, explain.

GOD'S PERSPECTIVE
Read the following Scripture passages and decide what they have to say about getting a good education.
• II Chronicles 1:10-12

• Proverbs 1:7; 2:10; 8:11

• Ecclesiastes 12:12

• Philippians 1:9-11

OPTIONAL ACTIVITY
• Talk to someone who is in a career field that you would like be in someday. Ask the person for advice on how to get a good education that will help you in this career.

SLAVES TO IGNORANCE

In the days of slavery in the South, slaves were denied the right to read or write. The slave owners didn't want the slaves to have an education because they knew that they could control their slaves if the slaves remained ignorant of the truth. They knew that there was power in education. Slaves were severely punished if they were caught reading. As a result, the slaves developed "pit schools"—holes in the ground where they would hide and study by candle-light. Even though they were threatened with having their fingers cut off, or having one of their eyes plucked out, they risked everything so that they could learn to read and write.
How badly do *you* want to learn?

CHOOSING A CAREER

"Whatever you do, work at it with all your heart, as working for the Lord, not for men" (Colossians 3:23).

One of the biggest decisions you will ever make is choosing a career. Some people wait a long time before they choose a career, but the smart ones begin thinking early about what they want to do with their lives and how they will achieve their career goals. It's normal to change your mind or to change careers, but it's best to at least get started on one particular career choice.

In the New Testament, the Greek word for "work" and "worship" can be the same word. In God's view, our work is something we do for Him, not for ourselves (Colossians 3:23). Many young people believe that we work simply to earn a living—so that we can have money and pay our bills. According to Scripture, we work to serve the Lord and to serve others, and our work then becomes an act of worship. In reality, God is the one who provides our living for us—usually in the form of a paycheck.

Let's find out what goes into choosing a career.

What are you good at?

What do you like to do?

What experience do you have?

What is you opinion of "work"? Check the following statements that you agree with.

_____ I love to work.

_____ If you are rich, you shouldn't have to work.

_____ Work is really boring.

_____ I work better alone than with other people.

_____ I like to work outside, rather than inside.

_____ I prefer to work with my hands, rather than my brain.

Why do you think having a career is important? Rate the following reasons from 1 (extremely important) to 11 (not important at all).

_____ To make a living

_____ To use the talents and abilities that I have

_____ To make my parents happy

_____ To make myself happy

_____ To make God happy

_____ To make the world a better place

_____ To keep me off the streets and off welfare

_____ To get rich

_____ To prevent boredom

_____ To serve God and others

_____ To achieve status in the community

SOME SAMPLE CAREERS

Teacher, police officer, doctor, lawyer, athlete, coach, accountant, politician, nurse, mail carrier, dentist, youth worker, sportscaster, newscaster, pastor, real estate agent, business owner, pilot, dancer, firefighter, social worker, scientist, cosmetologist, probation officer, engineer, car salesperson, mortician, insurance broker, carpenter, computer programmer

SOME KEY WORDS

Vocation—This is what you believe God has called you to do. It is your "mission statement." Example: "My *vocation* is to help people, especially children, learn and become productive members of society."

Career—This is how you will accomplish your vocation. Example: "I have chosen a *career* in education."

Occupation—This is the particular way you pursue your career and make a living. Example: "My *occupation* is teaching."

Job—This is the specific work that you do in your occupation. Example: "My *job* is teaching seventh graders at Memorial Middle School."

Write down a career that you would like to pursue.

Why did you choose this particular career?

Who do you know who has this career?

What steps can you take right now to prepare yourself for this career?

GOD'S PERSPECTIVE

Look up the following Scripture passages. See what they have to say about choosing a career.

- Ecclesiastes 5:18-20

- Matthew 6:25-34

- Matthew 9:35-38

- John 6:27

OPTIONAL ACTIVITY

• Visit some people who are working at the career you have chosen. Ask them questions about their career—what they enjoy about it and what they don't enjoy. If possible, spend some time with them "on the job" to see what the career is like. Find out if they have any advice for you.

THE FUTURE

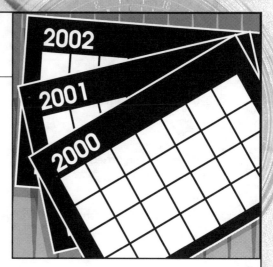

"Forgetting what is behind and straining toward what is ahead, I press on toward the goal to win the prize" (Philippians 3:13, 14).

I conducted a class for a group of about fifteen kids who had been suspended from an inner-city school in San Diego. I asked them what they wanted to be when they got older. Almost 75% of them said, "I don't know." It was so frustrating and sad to see so many young people without a clue regarding their future.

I asked them what would happen to me if I walked through their neighborhood not knowing where I was going. They all immediately yelled, "Man, you would get robbed or shot. You wouldn't make it back alive!" I said to them, "Well, if you don't know where you are going with your life, the same thing will happen to you. The world is a lot more dangerous than your neighborhood!"

Complete the following sentences.

- Ten years from now, the world will be . . .
    ____ better than it is now.
    ____ worse than it is now.
    ____ no different than it is now.

- When I think of my future, I . . .
    ____ feel discouraged.
    ____ get excited.
    ____ don't care.

- When I grow up, I want to be . . .
    ____ rich.
    ____ famous.
    ____ happy.

What occupation do you think you will have when you're older? Circle one of the occupations listed below or write in one of your own.
    Owner of small business
    Professional athlete
    Professional musician
    Garbage collector
    Social worker
    Stockbroker
    Schoolteacher
    Store clerk
    Accountant
    Housewife or househusband
    Corporation executive
    Astronaut
    Youth minister/pastor
    Writer/journalist
    Construction worker
    Police officer
    Nurse
    Entertainer
    Military officer
    Politician
    Other: _____

DREAM BIG: Think about yourself and the future. What do you think your life will be like . . .

- One year from now?
    Where will you live?

    What will you be doing?

    Will you be married or single?

    What accomplishments will you have achieved?

- Five years from now?
  Where will you live?

  What will you be doing?

  Will you be married or single?

  What accomplishments will you have achieved?

- Ten years from now?
  Where will you live?

  What will you be doing?

  Will you be married or single?

  What accomplishments will you have achieved?

True or false?

____ Today is the first day of the rest of your life.

____ God can help you achieve the things in life that you want to achieve.

____ There isn't much you can do to control your destiny.

____ The sky's the limit for people who have ambition and desire.

____ Your past determines your future.

____ There are too many problems to overcome in order to be successful in life.

____ A long journey begins with one small step.

____ You can't really plan the future. It's determined by chance or luck.

____ Christians have a positive outlook on the future because they are forgiven for the past.

____ The world is probably coming to an end in your lifetime.

____ Your hope for the future is based on your faith in God.

____ It's the government's job to provide a secure future for you.

____ You can do all things through Christ who gives you strength.

What are some steps you can take now to prepare for the future?

1.

2.

3.

GOD'S PERSPECTIVE

Read the following Scripture passages. See what they have to say about the future.

- Proverbs 19:21

- Matthew 6:25-34

- Luke 12:16-20

- I Corinthians 13:12

- Philippians 4:12, 13

- James 4:13-17

OPTIONAL ACTIVITIES

- Visit someone who is involved in one of the occupations that you're interested in. Find out what you need to do in order to prepare yourself for the future.

- Visit someone who is in need (perhaps someone in a hospital or a homeless shelter) and offer them some words of encouragement about the future.

SEX AND DATING

"The Lord God said, 'It is not good for the man to be alone. I will make a helper suitable for him'" (Genesis 2:18).

"Daughters of Jerusalem, I charge you: Do not arouse or awaken love until it so desires" (Song of Songs 8:4).

I had my first girlfriend, Pat, when I was eleven years old. I really thought I was in love. She was my steady girl. I had no idea how to act around her, but I just knew she was my girl. That is, until I met her cousin a few months later. I fell in love with Pat's cousin and dated her even though she lived four hours away. I just knew she was the one I would love forever. But as it turned out, there was another girl a few months later and someone else after that. I had no idea what dating was all about.

Neither do kids today. Many kids think dating is basically spending time with a person you like until he or she becomes the person you start having sex with. Dating for many kids is just a warm-up for a sexual encounter. Is that what you think?

Here are some facts about dating. First, the main purpose of dating is to learn how to relate to a person of the opposite sex in a positive way. Dating should help you learn to treat another person with dignity and respect. Second, dating is not mandatory. Many people don't start dating until they are in college. Third, dating doesn't have to be "romantic." Some of the best dates are fun times—going to ball games, parties, or school functions together. Fourth, dating is often best in groups—a bunch of guys and girls going out and having fun together.

Christian dating adds another dimension. Dating is also a time to help another person grow strong in his or her faith. If the person you are dating isn't helping you grow in the Lord, then you are definitely with the wrong person.

What do you think is the perfect thing to do on a date? Write a short description of the "perfect date."

ANCIENT DATING

Many years ago, young men and women practiced an ancient ritual called dating. The male talked to a female at school or on the way home from school. When the male was sure that female knew who he was, he would call and ask her to go out on a "date." The date might involve going to a dance or movie. The boy and girl would attend the entire event together, go out afterward for a Coke and fries, and then go home fairly early. Often the dates were during the day and involved a picnic or an afternoon in the park.

Almost always, the female would have to get permission from her parents first, and the male would have to meet her parents before the date. Dating was practiced by kids who were at least 16, and the male asked the female, never the other way around. Most dates were "double dates" with two couples. Very little sex, if any, was involved. Usually there was lots of talking, having fun, holding hands, an arm around the girl, and maybe a good-night kiss at the door.

—From *Teaching the Truth about Sex* by Mike Yaconelli and David Lynn (Youth Specialties)

Complete the following sentence with the three best answers.

I would like to date a person who . . .

____ is really good-looking.

____ has a lot of money.

____ is a strong Christian.

____ has sexual experience.

____ treats me with respect.

____ has a reputation for being "wild."

____ has a sense of humor.

____ likes the same things I do.

____ is very intelligent and gets good grades.

____ goes to my church.

____ is popular with all of the other kids.

____ likes to "get physical" right away.

____ won't date anyone else but me.

____ has a great personality.

Do you agree or disagree with the following statements?

A D You shouldn't start dating until you are old enough to drive.

A D Couples should share expenses on dates.

A D Most kids today expect to have sex on dates.

A D It's OK to get physical on a date so long as you don't have sexual intercourse.

A D Christians should pray on a date.

A D Having sex draws people closer together.

A D Christians should only date other Christians.

A D It's OK for girls to ask guys out on a date.

A D It's not cool to be a virgin.

A D Parents should approve of the person you are dating.

A D A person should date many people, not just one.

A D You should take condoms on every date, just in case.

When do you think is the right time to have sexual intercourse?

____ When the other person gives his or her consent

____ When you "feel the urge"

____ When you've made a commitment to each other

____ When you know for sure that you are in love

____ When you've taken the proper precautions to avoid pregnancy or sexually transmitted diseases

____ When you know for sure that this is the person you will marry

____ When you are married

____ When the mood is right

____ Whenever you want

GOD'S PERSPECTIVE

Read the following Scripture passages. See what they have to say about sex and dating.

• I Corinthians 6:18-20

• Ephesians 5:1-3

• I Thessalonians 4:3-8

TEN REASONS TO CHOOSE SEXUAL ABSTINENCE

1. Abstinence is the only method of birth control that is 100% guaranteed.
2. Abstinence is the only guaranteed method of avoiding sexually transmitted diseases.
3. Abstinence allows a couple to deepen their relationship in other ways.
4. Abstinence can be a test of true love. True love waits.
5. Abstinence is a test of moral character.
6. Abstinence is a test of personal responsibility and self-control.
7. Abstinence reduces the pain of a broken relationship.
8. Abstinence allows you to save yourself for the person you marry.
9. Abstinence reduces sexual pressure in a relationship.
10. Abstinence is God's will for people who are not married.

OPTIONAL ACTIVITIES

• Interview your parents or some other adults about their dating experiences when they were young. Find out what they did right and what they did wrong.

• Go to a Christian bookstore and ask for a good book on sex and dating for teenagers. If you can, buy one and read it.

MORALITY

"And what does the Lord require of you? To act justly and to love mercy and to walk humbly with your God" (Micah 6:8).

I was in Austin, Texas, speaking at some schools when I was confronted with a very sad situation. Before the assembly started, the principal told me about two students who were playing with a gun. One kid held it in his mouth thinking there were no bullets in the gun. As they joked around, the boy pulled the trigger. The gun went off, killing him instantly in front of his close friend.

The surviving boy was at school that day and I had a chance to talk with him. He told me about all of the things they were accustomed to doing. Both of these guys were troublemakers in the community. They had a habit of cutting school, picking on younger kids, vandalizing the neighborhood, getting drunk, and doing drugs. As we talked, he began to cry as he realized that his life was going in the wrong direction. It took the death of a friend for him to realize that he was living a life that was immoral and deadly.

Immorality ultimately leads to death. There is no way to escape it. "The wages of sin is death," Paul says in Romans 6:23. Unfortunately, too many young people don't discover this until it is too late.

Who or what do you think is the ultimate authority in determining what is right and wrong?

For you?	For most people?	
_____	_____	The Bible
_____	_____	The law of the land
_____	_____	Parents
_____	_____	Friends
_____	_____	The media (TV, movies, music)
_____	_____	Role models (athletes, movie stars, entertainers)
_____	_____	Self
_____	_____	Other: _____

True or false?

_____ It doesn't matter what you do, as long as it doesn't hurt anybody else.

_____ The Ten Commandments are obsolete.

_____ Most teenagers think it's dumb to live by the rules.

_____ Guys are more immoral than girls.

_____ Most people know the difference between right and wrong.

_____ It's hard to do the right thing when all of your friends don't.

_____ Sometimes it's OK to break the law.

_____ Most kids think it's cool to be "bad."

_____ If you do break the law, the important thing is to not get caught.

_____ "Eat, drink, and be merry, for tomorrow you may die."

_____ Do unto others before they do it unto you.

_____ Let your conscience be your guide.

_____ Everybody lives an immoral life, so it's really no big deal.

_____ Christians aren't perfect, just forgiven.

_____ I would live a better life if I could.

Which of the following moral issues are sometimes a big problem for you? for your friends?

For you?	For your friends?	
_____	_____	Cheating on tests
_____	_____	Reckless driving
_____	_____	Sexual behavior
_____	_____	Lying to parents
_____	_____	Using bad language
_____	_____	Stealing
_____	_____	Doing drugs or alcohol
_____	_____	Vandalizing, tagging, destroying other people's property
_____	_____	Disobeying parents
_____	_____	Looking at pornography
_____	_____	Violent behavior (fighting, carrying, or using weapons)
_____	_____	Other: _____

The following are several reasons people give for living according to high moral standards. Which ones make good sense to you?

_____ You will live a happier life.
_____ You will live a longer life.
_____ You will please your parents.
_____ You will please God.
_____ You will be more successful in life.
_____ People will admire you.
_____ You won't end up in jail.
_____ You will set a good example for younger children.
_____ You will go to heaven when you die.
_____ You will have a clear conscience.
_____ Other: _____

How can bad people become good people?
_____ They can't.
_____ They should stop being bad and try to be good.
_____ They should get a good job.
_____ They should go to church once in a while.
_____ They should see a psychiatrist.
_____ They should move to a new neighborhood.
_____ They should read the Bible.
_____ They should ask God to change them from the inside out.

Jesus told His followers that the two most important rules to live by were these:
1. Love God.
2. Love other people.

Do you think you could live by those two rules? Which one do you think is harder? Why?

Jesus also said, "Do unto others as you would have them do unto you." If you lived that way, how would your life be different?

GOD'S PERSPECTIVE
Read the following Scripture passages. See what they have to do with morality.
- Romans 3:23

- Romans 6:23

- Ephesians 2:1-5

- I John 1:9

- I John 2:15-17

OPTIONAL ACTIVITY
- Watch several of your favorite TV shows and determine whether the actions portrayed are right or wrong. Give a point for every right action; subtract a point for every wrong action.

ANGER AND VIOLENCE

"A fool gives full vent to his anger, but a wise man keeps himself under control" (Proverbs 29:11).

I had a rather heated discussion one day with members of a local gang about gang violence. They were trying to convince me that they had no choice but to be violent and kill people. If a person wore the colors of a rival gang, made threats against them, or made physical contact, then they said they had no choice but to shoot him or her.

I proceeded to tell the leader of this gang that I was going to hit him for saying what he did, and I wanted to see how he would respond. I hit him three times in the chest. He just stood there. He didn't hit me once. He said he wouldn't hit me because I was a "preacher." I told him that the real reason he didn't hit me was that he had made a decision beforehand not to hit me. He could make that same decision anytime he decided to make it.

Nobody is forced to be violent. You have power over your anger. There's nothing wrong with being angry, but you can decide how to respond to that anger. Violence is a choice that we make.

List three things that really make you angry.

1.

2.

3.

Complete the following sentence.
When I get angry, I . . .

Yes or no?

Y   N   It's wrong to get angry.

Y   N   I have a right to be angry when someone hurts me.

Y   N   I don't get mad; I get even.

Y   N   When I get mad, I should deal with it right away.

Y   N   People who lose their tempers are immature.

There are many different ways to deal with anger. Which of the following ways do you think are OK for you?

_____ Get even; do unto others what they did unto you

_____ Yell and scream

_____ Say hurtful things to the person who made you angry

_____ Cry

_____ Forget about it

_____ Inflict physical harm on whoever made you angry

_____ Throw things

_____ Pray

_____ Cool off for a while; then decide what to do

_____ Take it out on someone else

_____ Pretend it didn't happen

_____ Confront the person who made you angry and talk about it

_____ Buy a gun

_____ Walk away

_____ Other: _____

Put a + sign next to all of the above responses that produce positive (good) results. Put a – sign next to those responses that produce negative (bad) results.

How would you respond to the following situations? Choose from the previous list of responses or come up with some of your own.

1. Someone calls you a name.

2. Your parents blame you for something that you didn't do.

3. Someone steals something out of your locker at school.

4. Someone cuts in front of you in line.

5. Someone threatens a member of your family.

6. You are angry with yourself.

List three positive ways to express your anger.

1.

2.

3.

GOD'S PERSPECTIVE

Read the following Scripture passages. See what they have to say about anger and violence.

• Proverbs 14:17

• Matthew 6:14, 15

• Ephesians 4:26

OPTIONAL ACTIVITIES

• Look through a newspaper to see how many examples of angry people you can find. How did they deal with their anger?

• Talk to a police officer about anger and violence. Ask the officer how he or she keeps his or her cool under fire.

• Go to a courtroom to observe the trial of someone who has been accused of a violent crime.

• Practice "walking away" from problems for one week. Say "I'm sorry" even when it's not your fault. Note what happens when you do this.

ALCOHOL

"Do not get drunk on wine. . . . Instead, be filled with the Spirit" (Ephesians 5:18).

Many people associate drinking with having a good time. "Let's party" for a lot of kids means "Let's get drunk!" When I was in college, I was a resident advisor for a dorm. One night a student was out drinking and came to bed drunk. In the middle of the night, some students came knocking on my door because they thought the student was dead.

He wasn't dead, but when I found him, he had vomited in his sleep and his vomit had dried as it ran from his mouth to his pillow. He was a mess. The students wanted me to clean him up because they couldn't stand to leave him in that condition. But there was nothing I could do for him. I just left him there, figuring he could clean up his own mess when he woke up.

There is nothing anyone can do for you if you decide to get wasted on alcohol. Eventually you will wind up with vomit on your face. Before you start drinking booze, you had better consider the consequences. Alcohol is a destroyer of people's lives.

On a scale of 1 to 10, what is your opinion of alcohol?

1	2	3	4	5	6	7	8	9	10
It's Bad for You				It's Neither Good nor Bad					It'sGood for You

When do you think it's OK to drink alcohol?

____ Never

____ At parties

____ When you need to relax

____ At dinner (with food)

____ Communion at church

____ When you're thirsty

____ With friends

____ When you're legally old enough

____ When your parents give you permission

____ Anytime, with moderation

____ Only at home

Do you agree or disagree with the following statements?

A   D   Drinking alcohol is better than doing drugs.

A   D   There is nothing wrong with drinking as long as you don't get drunk.

A   D   If you don't drink, you won't be able to have a social life.

A   D   Everybody should get drunk at least once, just to see what it's like.

A   D   It should be legal for teenagers to drink beer and wine.

A   D   Some people can hold their liquor better than others.

Check the following sentences that apply to you.

____ I have never drunk alcohol; I couldn't tell you what it tastes like.

____ I tried alcohol to see what it tastes like, but that's all.

____ I drink alcohol once in a while, but I don't get drunk.

____ I have gotten drunk on alcohol.

____ I drink too much.

____ Some people in my family have alcohol problems.

____ I knew someone who was killed by a drunk driver.

____ I know someone who is an alcoholic.

____ Alcohol has made me do some stupid things.

____ I plan to stay away from alcohol for the rest of my life.

Which of the following statements makes the most sense to you? Explain.
1. "If you drink, don't drive."
2. "If you drive, don't drink."

Why do you think most people drink?
____ They want to get high.
____ They want to be cool.
____ They want to relieve stress.
____ They like the taste of alcohol.
____ It's hereditary.
____ They have a drinking problem.
____ They want to increase their sex drive.
____ Their friends drink.
____ Other: _____

> According to one survey of teenagers, these are the top reasons why teenagers drink alcohol:
> 70% Friends who drink
> 48% Parents who drink
> 29% Desire to be grown up
> 14% Relatives who drink
> 12% Seeing people drink on TV
> 10% Desire to be "cool"
> 8% Advertising
> 2% Don't know why
> —From *Youthworker Update*, January 1993

If someone offers you a drink at a party, you should . . .
____ Say, "Thanks," and drink it.
____ Carry it around for a while, then dump it in the toilet.
____ Say, "No thanks."
____ Give the person a lecture on the evils of drinking alcohol.
____ Drink it slowly so that it won't affect you so much.
____ Ask if there are any nonalcoholic drinks being served.
____ Other: _____

GOD'S PERSPECTIVE
Read the following Scripture passages and decide what they have to say about drinking alcohol.
• Isaiah 5:11, 12

• John 2:1-11

• Romans 14:21

• I Corinthians 6:12, 13

OPTIONAL ACTIVITIES
• Visit a meeting of Alcoholics Anonymous. They take place almost every night of the week somewhere in your community. Call ahead of time to make arrangements to attend and observe a meeting.

• Visit a homeless shelter or a rescue mission and interview some street people about their experiences with alcohol. Tell them that you are compiling advice on alcohol use for teenagers and you would like their comments.

• Get information on SADD (Students Against Drunk Driving). For information, call 508-481-3568.

DRUGS

"Be self-controlled and alert. Your enemy the devil prowls around like a roaring lion looking for someone to devour" (I Peter 5:8).

Why do you think so many kids try drugs?

____ To see what it feels like

____ Peer pressure

____ To get high

____ To make them feel sexier

____ It's a fad

____ They don't realize what they're doing

____ Drugs are easy to get

____ It's cool

____ To escape from reality

____ Other: _____

In your school, what percentage of the students do you think use drugs on a regular basis? (Circle one.)

0%   10%   20%   30%   40%   50%

60%   70%   80%   90%   100%

If you could talk to a third-grade class about drug abuse, what would you tell them? Think of three main points that you would make.

1.

2.

3.

Do you agree or disagree with the following statements?

A   D   The dangers of experimenting with drugs far outweigh the benefits of trying them.

A   D   If you try drugs just once, you will be hooked.

A   D   Drugs can have a positive influence on a person's life as well as a negative one.

A   D   If one of my friends offered me drugs, then that person would no longer be a friend.

A   D   Occasional drug use is not harmful.

A   D   Drinking alcohol is just as bad as doing drugs.

A   D   My parents probably used drugs when they were my age.

A   D   Not all drugs are addictive.

A   D   Drugs should be legalized.

Which of the following drugs do you think are OK for teenagers to try?

____ Tobacco (nicotine)

____ Heroin

____ Cough syrup

____ Cocaine

____ Model-airplane glue

____ Marijuana

____ Coffee (caffeine)

____ Alcohol

____ Toad licking

____ SD

____ Anabolic steroids

____ Methamphetamines

____ Ecstasy

____ Other: _____

____ None of the above

> "We have a lot of young fans and I don't want to have anything to do with encouraging drug use. People who promote drug use are [expletive]. I chose to do drugs. I don't feel sorry for myself at all, but I have nothing good to say about drugs. They are a total waste of time."
>
> —Kurt Cobain, lead singer of the rock group Nirvana, from a 1992 interview in the *Los Angeles Times*. Cobain committed suicide in 1994.

The following are some "pros" and "cons" regarding drug use. Which do you think are the most persuasive? Can you think of others?

Pros

Drugs make you feel good for a while.

Drugs make you less inhibited.

Drugs are cool.

Drugs can sometimes relieve pain or depression.

Drugs are dangerous and I like living "on the edge."

Other: _____

Cons

Drugs can cause brain damage, heart failure, and can kill you.

The high you get from drugs is only temporary, then you crash.

Most drugs are illegal, and using them can get you thrown in jail.

Drugs are expensive.

Drugs are addictive and hard to stop using.

Other: _____

GOD'S PERSPECTIVE

Read the following Scripture passages. See what they have to say about using drugs.

- Romans 12:1, 2

- I Corinthians 3:16, 17

- I Corinthians 10:13

- I Corinthians 10:31

OPTIONAL ACTIVITY

• Visit a drug rehabilitation center. Talk to some of the doctors and assistants who work there. Find out how many teenagers are involved in treatment. Ask for some literature on drug abuse.

MONEY

"Choose my instruction instead of silver, knowledge rather than choice gold" (Proverbs 8:10).

One day a guy in a Rolls Royce pulled up to a traffic light next to a sports car. The guy in the sports car yelled out the window to the guy in the Rolls, "You think you're cool in that Rolls, don't you?" The guy in the Rolls said, "Yeah, sure. This is a $150,000 car." The guy in the sports car said, "Do you have a phone in that Rolls?" "Yes, I do," said the guy in the Rolls. "Well, so do I," said the guy in the sports car. "Do you have a TV?" "Yes, I do," said the guy in the Rolls. "Well, do you have a bed in your car?" The guy in the Rolls paused for a moment and said, "No, I don't have a bed in my car." The guy in the sports car drove off laughing as loud as he could.

The guy in the Rolls was steaming mad. He went out and had a queen-size bed installed in the back of his Rolls Royce. Then he went looking for the guy in the sports car. When he finally found the guy at his home, he banged on the window and woke him up. "What do you want?," said the owner of the sports car. "Remember me?" asked the guy with the Rolls Royce. "Yeah, you're the guy with the Rolls Royce with no bed," said the sports car owner. "Well, I'm here to inform you," said the guy with the Rolls, "that I have installed a queen-size bed in the back of my car!" The guy with the sports car started laughing. "You woke me up for that? That's the dumbest thing I've ever heard of! A bed in a Rolls Royce!"

If you think that having money is what makes you somebody, then you'll never be anybody at all—because no matter how much money you have, or how much stuff you accumulate, you will never have enough.

How important is money to you?

1	2	3	4	5	6	7	8	9	10

Not important
at all

Extremely
important

How do you spend your money? Estimate some percentages so that your total adds up to 100%.

____ Clothes

____ Food

____ Entertainment (movies, parties, etc.)

____ Personal stuff (tapes, CDs, makeup, toys)

____ Car

____ Insurance

____ Living expenses (rent, utilities, etc.)

____ Helping with family expenses

____ Education (books, etc.)

____ Savings/investments

____ Giving to the church or to charities

____ Taxes

____ Other: _____

____ Other: _____

How do you think those percentages will change as you get older? Put a + sign next to those items that will increase as you get older and a − sign next to those that will get smaller.

Check the statements below that best describe your present financial situation.

____ I have enough money.

____ I'm broke most of the time.

____ My family has a lot of money.

____ My family has money problems.

____ I deserve more money than I'm getting right now.

_____ I waste a lot of money.

_____ I'm jealous of other people my age who have more money than I do.

_____ I have a budget that I live by.

_____ I worry a lot about money.

_____ When I get a lot of money, I feel a lot better.

_____ I'm saving money right now to buy something that I really want.

True or false?

_____ Money is the root of all evil.

_____ A fool and his money are soon parted.

_____ The golden rule is "He who has the gold rules."

_____ Money gives you power.

_____ Being rich is a blessing from God.

_____ "Blessed are the poor" is not a very practical concept today.

_____ No one should have more money than he or she needs.

_____ If you don't need money, then you don't need to work.

_____ There is a difference between "needs" and "wants."

_____ Most teenagers today have too much money.

_____ Athletes and entertainers who make millions are greedy.

_____ Once you get rich, you will be happy.

_____ It's wrong for Christians to be rich.

_____ No one should get money unless he or she earns it.

_____ It's a sin to spend all of your money on yourself.

GOD'S PERSPECTIVE

Read the following Scripture passages. See what they have to say about money.

- Proverbs 11:4

- Proverbs 30:8, 9

- Malachi 3:8-10

- Matthew 16:26

- Matthew 25:14-30

- Mark 10:25

OPTIONAL ACTIVITIES

- Work out a budget for the next month and live by it.

- Figure out your "net worth" in terms of money. Is this really what you are worth?

- Set up an appointment with a very wealthy person. Ask him or her questions about the relationship between money and happiness. Visit some people who are poor and ask them the same questions.

RACISM

"There is neither Jew nor Greek, slave nor free, male nor female, for you are all one in Christ Jesus" (Galatians 3:28).

When I was nineteen years old, I had the opportunity to work in northern Maine as a surveyor. We hired a local teenager named Robby to help us do the work. He spent about ten days with us. We did everything together. We hung out together, slept in the same room, and ate meals together. One day we were walking through the woods and Robby said something rather interesting to me. He said he had never met an African-American person in his whole life. I thought this was interesting because he seemed so at ease around me, an African-American man. The more we talked, the more I realized that he hadn't been taught to be prejudiced. He was like a child when it came to such things. He was willing to learn and not make snap judgments based on small bits of information. Robby's ignorance—not to race, but to racism—was a great blessing.

Racists base their views of a group of people on a few experiences or a little information from rumors they have heard from others. Just as I hope my friendship and experience with Robby will help him get along with people different from himself, I hope you will be open to meeting different types of people and giving yourself a chance to make new friends.

Yes or no?

Y N Have you ever had someone treat you unfairly because of the way you looked?

Y N Have you ever avoided someone because of his or her race?

Y N Do you have any close friends of another race?

Y N Do you ever tell jokes that make fun of people of another race?

Y N Do you think there are some races that are superior to others?

Y N Do you have family members who are prejudiced against another race?

Y N Would you feel comfortable in a church with a pastor of a different race than you?

Y N Do you think it's OK to date someone of a different race?

Y N Do you think it's OK to marry someone of a different race?

Y N Do you think racism is still a big problem in this country?

Why do you think people are racists?

____ Because they are ignorant

____ Because they are afraid

____ Because of their upbringings

____ Because people of other races have hurt them in some way

____ Because they have a need to feel superior to others

____ Because they are influenced by the media to hate other people

____ Because they are convinced that certain kinds of people are inferior

____ Because of grudges from the past (wars, slavery, land-stealing, etc.)

____ Because they are sinners

On the following "racist scale," how would you rate . . .

Yourself?

1	2	3	4	5	6	7	8	9	10

Not Racist   Very Racist

Your family?

1	2	3	4	5	6	7	8	9	10

Not Racist   Very Racist

Your school?

1	2	3	4	5	6	7	8	9	10

Not Racist   Very Racist

Your church?

1	2	3	4	5	6	7	8	9	10

Not Racist   Very Racist

GOD'S PERSPECTIVE

Read the following Scripture passages to see what they have to say about racism.

- I Samuel 16:7

- Matthew 7:1-5

- Ephesians 2:19-22

- James 2:8, 9

- I John 2:9-11; 3:10; 4:20

NOTE: If you can't call people of different races "brother" or "sister," then you can't pray "Our Father . . ."

OPTIONAL ACTIVITIES

• Visit a neighborhood that is predominantly of a different race. Write down everything that you feel inside—the fears you have, the reasons you think you feel that way, and so on. What are the differences and similarities you notice about what's going on?

• Go to a church that is predominantly of a different race. See what differences and similarities there are between that church experience and your own.

• Try to make a friend at school who is of a different race.

GOD

"Yet for us there is but one God, the Father, from whom all things came and for whom we live" (I Corinthians 8:6).

When we read the newspapers and watch the news on TV, we are seeing more and more teenagers involved in more and more violent crimes. Many people have theories for this rise in teen violence—boredom, lack of family support, low self-esteem, violence on TV and in movies. But what is the real deal?

I believe much of the violence we see comes from a denial of authority. Not the authority of police, teachers, or even parents, but the authority of God. Young people today have lost a fear of God because they don't know who He is. When I talk about the fear of God, I don't mean being afraid of God. Instead, the fear of God comes from being aware of who God is, what He wants from us, and what His feelings are toward us. When we truly come to know God, we are able to have a positive relationship with Him that gives our lives direction, purpose, and meaning.

When I was playing in the NFL, our coaches would try to instill in us a healthy fear of the next team on our schedule each week. That didn't mean we were afraid of the other team; it just meant that we respected them enough to play up to our abilities. It would enable us to practice hard, be a disciplined football team, and live up to the expectations of our coaches and fans on game day.

In the same way, a healthy fear of God enables us to live up to our potential, avoid making mistakes, and ultimately be winners in life.

What is your belief about God?
____ I don't believe there is a God.
____ I believe that God is like the "Force" in the *Star Wars* movies.
____ I believe that God created the world, but doesn't involve Himself in our daily lives.
____ I believe that God knows me and loves me.
____ I believe that God looks like an old man with a white beard.
____ I believe that all religions serve the same God.
____ I don't believe that you can know for sure that there is a God.

____ I believe that the Bible is God's Word to us.
____ I believe that scientific discoveries like evolution prove that God doesn't exist.
____ I believe that it is possible to have a personal relationship with God.
____ I believe that God is probably angry with me.
____ I believe that God causes all of the bad things that happen to people.
____ I believe that Jesus Christ is God.

Which of the following words best describe God to you? (Circle as many as you wish.)

Eternal   Powerful   Distant   Loving   Kind

Angry   Cruel   Remote   Generous   Mysterious

Patient   Busy   Dead   Good   Forgiving

Punishing   Wise   Dependable   Irrelevant   Scary

True or false?
____ If you know about God, then you know God.
____ It is impossible to know for sure that there is a God.
____ People who "hear God speak" are crazy.
____ I wish I had a better understanding of God.
____ If you want to know what God is like, take a look at Jesus Christ.
____ When you pray, God listens to what you have to say.
____ Pastors and priests know God better than other people do.

____ God reveals Himself to us through other people.

____ If God really does exist, then what He has to say must be pretty important.

____ The only way to know God personally is to be a Christian.

____ I wish I were closer to God.

The best way to learn about God is to . . . (check the best answer)

____ Go to church

____ Read the Bible

____ Talk to a minister or priest

____ Pray

____ Believe in Jesus Christ

____ All of the above

Jesus Christ used a story to describe what God is like. The parable of the lost son is found in Luke 15:11-32. What do you think Jesus wanted us to know about God from this story?

THE BLIND MEN AND THE ELEPHANT

A famous parable is told of a village where all of the people were blind. One day, six men from that village were on the road when they came upon a man who was riding an elephant. The men asked the rider if he would allow them to touch the great beast, because although they had heard about elephants, they had never been close to one. They wanted to be able to go back to their village and tell the other villagers what an elephant looked like. The rider agreed and led each of the six men to a different part of the elephant. They each touched and felt until they were certain that they knew what the animal looked like.

When they returned to their village, the villagers gathered around to hear about the elephant.

The first man, who had felt the animal's side, said, "An elephant is like a great thick wall."

"Nonsense," said the second man, who had felt the elephant's tusk. "He is rather short, round, and smooth, but very sharp. I would compare an elephant not with a wall, but with a spear!"

The third man, who had touched the ear, joined in. "It is nothing at all like a wall or a spear," he said. "It is like a gigantic leaf made of thick wool carpet. It moves when you touch it."

"I disagree," said the fourth man, who had handled the trunk. "I can tell you that an elephant is like a giant snake." The fifth man shouted his disapproval. He had touched one of the elephant's legs and concluded, "An elephant is round and thick, like a tree."

The sixth man had been allowed to ride on the elephant's back, and he protested, "Can none of you accurately describe an elephant? Clearly he is like a gigantic moving mountain!"

To this day, the men continue to argue, and no one in the village has any idea what an elephant looks like.

The Bible describes God in many different ways because He is experienced in many different ways. He is the Creator of the Universe, but He is also the Faithful Friend. He is the Righteous Judge, but He is also the Forgiving Father. For us to understand God, or for us to understand the Bible, we must take the Word of God in its entirety and study it carefully. Whenever we get only one view of God, or one perspective on the truth, we are likely to be misled.

GOD'S PERSPECTIVE

Read the following Scripture passages to see what they have to say about God.

• Deuteronomy 32:4

• Psalm 19:1

• Psalm 23

• Psalm 118:29

• Matthew 7:11

• Romans 11:33-36

OPTIONAL ACTIVITIES

• Go to a mountain or some other scenic place where it is possible to enjoy the beauty of nature. Take some time there to meditate on the greatness of God.

• Spend an hour in a quiet chapel or church reading psalms and listening to God.

• Write a letter to God.

• Write a letter as if it were a letter from God to you.

JESUS CHRIST

"He is the image of the invisible God, the firstborn over all creation" (Colossians 1:15).

For many years I watched the late Lyle Alzado play football. He played for several NFL teams and was always portrayed as a ferocious guy who would bite your head off.

One summer I was working out in a gym, getting ready for the upcoming football season. I approached the weights to bench press. I looked up. There was Lyle Alzado, the mean monster who was playing for our archrivals, the L.A. Raiders, at the time. I suddenly wondered how he would respond to me.

I said hello and asked him if I could work out with him and his partner. I fully expected a little attitude from him, but I got the total opposite. He was kind and gracious, a real gentleman. We worked out together the entire summer and developed a strong friendship. I discovered that Lyle Alzado had been misrepresented by the media. In reality, he was a gentle giant who cared a lot about people.

In the same way, Jesus Christ is often misrepresented by the world. What do you think of Him? Who is He, really? Before you pass judgment on Jesus, maybe you had better meet Him yourself.

"I Am"

Jesus made several statements about Himself that began with the words "I am . . ." Look up the following verses in the Bible and write the word or words that Jesus used to describe Himself.

John 6:35—"I am _____ ."
John 8:12—"I am _____ ."
John 10:9—"I am _____ ."
John 10:11—"I am _____ ."
John 11:25—"I am _____ ."
John 14:6—"I am _____ ."
John 15:1-5—"I am _____ ."

Which one of the "I am" statements above tells you the most about Jesus? Which one has been true for you?

The following are words that some people use to describe Jesus. Cross out the ones that you think are inaccurate.

Meek   Loving   Tough   Cool   Humble
Powerful   Strange   Friend   Embarrassing
Alive   Smart   God   Wimp   Mysterious   Fun
Sad   Judging   Dead   Hero

Pretend that Jesus is presently living in your community. Based on what you know about Him . . .
Where do you think He would live?

What style of clothes would He wear?

What do you think He would do on Friday or Saturday nights?

What kind of music would He like?

Who do you think He would hang out with?

Would most of your friends like Him?

Do you think you would like Him?

Which of the following statements do you agree with?

_____ Jesus was a wise man who taught people how to love each other.

_____ Faith in Jesus is the only way for a person to know God.

_____ Jesus was a very persuasive cult leader.

_____ Jesus was the only perfect human being who ever lived.

_____ Jesus rose from the grave and is alive today.

_____ Most of what we know about Jesus is mythology.

_____ If you believe in Jesus, then you try to live like Jesus did.

_____ Jesus was a great religious leader, like Mohammed or Buddha.

_____ Jesus died on the cross for the sins the world.

_____ Jesus was—and is—God in human flesh.

_____ If you believe in Jesus, you will go to heaven.

_____ Jesus is coming back to earth again.

_____ Jesus wasn't really human.

_____ It is possible for Jesus to make you into a new person.

Circle the number that best represents your relationship with Christ.

1   2   3   4   5   6   7   8   9   10
I feel far away from Jesus   I feel very close to Jesus

GOD'S PERSPECTIVE

Read the following Scripture passages to see what they have to say about Jesus Christ.

- Matthew 16:16

- John 1:1, 14

- John 3:16

- John 10:30

- Colossians 1:13-23

- Hebrews 4:14, 15

OPTIONAL ACTIVITIES

• Go to a video store. Rent the movie *Jesus of Nazareth*. Invite some friends over and watch it together.

• Read one of the Gospels (Matthew, Mark, Luke, or John) from start to finish. Use a modern translation that is easy for you to understand (like *The Message*, a translation by Eugene Peterson). Make a list of the important things you learn about Jesus from reading it.

THE BIBLE

"For the word of God is living and active" (Hebrews 4:12).

In 1983, during my second year with the San Diego Chargers, I decided to drive home to New York immediately after the team mini-camp in May.

It was about 2,700 miles, and I couldn't wait. Even though I knew New York was northeast of San Diego, I really didn't know the quickest way to get there. I didn't want to waste time driving places I didn't need to go, especially since I would be alone. I wanted to get home as soon as possible.

So I went to the Automobile Club (AAA) and got a "triptick"—a map of the country that had all of the roads and highways I needed to take highlighted with a yellow marker. The people at the Auto Club highlighted 2,700 miles of road—every highway, big and small. Even though there were many other roads on the map, they gave me the ones best for the trip that I was going to take.

I drove the entire distance in less than three days. I think I could have arrived even sooner, but I decided to try a shortcut that wasn't on the map and got lost. That shortcut was not only frustrating, but it cost me valuable time. Most of the trip was smooth and easy, even though I had never traveled that route before. I trusted the "triptick" completely and it got me to my destination without a hitch.

The Bible is our road map through life. There are many roads, but the Bible has marked out the decisions you need to make in order to make it safely home to God.

> The Bible has sixty-six books—1,089 chapters. It was written by more than forty people who lived on three different continents over a period of sixteen hundred years. Some were poor, some were rich, some were sad, happy, depressed, or full of joy. They wrote about hundreds of topics and they all agreed with each other.
>
> Do you consider this a coincidence or a miracle of God?

Which of the following phrases best describe the Bible? Check all those that are true. Put a star next to the one that you think is the "most true."

____ The Bible is a book primarily about God.
____ The Bible is a book of great literature.
____ The Bible is a history book.

____ The Bible is a love letter to us from God.
____ The Bible is a book of rules.
____ The Bible is a book of mythology.
____ The Bible is an instruction book for life.
____ The Bible is a book that contains a lot of wisdom and truth, but is not *completely* true.
____ The Bible is the Holy Word of God.

What is your favorite story from the Bible? Why?

Which of the following statements do you think are in the Bible?

____ 1. God helps those who help themselves.
____ 2. The Lord works in mysterious ways.
____ 3. I can do all things through Christ who gives me strength.
____ 4. All things work for good to those who love God.
____ 5. Cleanliness is next to godliness.
____ 6. Do unto others before they do it unto you.
____ 7. Don't judge others or you will be judged yourself.
____ 8. All men are created equal.
____ 9. Just say no.
____ 10. Man does not live on bread alone.

True or false?

____ Science has proven that the Bible is not true.
____ The Bible has answers to every problem you will face.
____ The Bible was written by people of God who were inspired by the Holy Spirit.

_____ Sometimes the Bible can be misinterpreted.
_____ The Bible is out-of-date and irrelevant to the modern world.
_____ Other books are just as important as the Bible.
_____ You should worship God, not the Bible.
_____ The Bible is the only book you need to read.

How often do you read the Bible?
_____ Never
_____ Rarely (about once a year)
_____ About once a month
_____ About once a week
_____ Almost every day

Complete the following sentence by checking one of the following words.
     When I read the Bible, I feel . . .
          _____ good.
          _____ guilty.
          _____ stupid.
          _____ bored.
          _____ excited.
          _____ confused.
          _____ informed.

Write your initials next to any of the following statements that apply to you.
     _____ I have my own Bible.
     _____ I have a translation of the Bible that I can understand.
     _____ I am embarrassed to carry a Bible to school.
     _____ I don't understand a lot of what I read in the Bible.
     _____ I look forward to reading the Bible.
     _____ When I have a problem, I look in the Bible for guidance and comfort.
     _____ I try to live according to what the Bible says.
     _____ I would like to read the Bible more than I do.

GOD'S PERSPECTIVE

Read the following Scripture passages to see what they have to say about the Bible.
• Psalm 119:9-11

• Matthew 24:35

• II Timothy 2:15

• Hebrews 4:12

• James 1:21-24

OPTIONAL ACTIVITIES

• Go to a Christian bookstore. Check out all of the different kinds of Bibles that are available today. Compare the different translations to see if there is one that you like better than the others.

• Pick a book of the Bible (like the Gospel of John) and read through it this month. Try to read a little every day. Write down all of the best verses or thoughts that you discover from your reading.

The Prince of Grenada, an heir to the Spanish Crown, was sentenced to life in solitary confinement in Madrid's ancient prison called "the place of the skull" because it was so fearful, dirty, and dreary inside. Everyone knew that once you were in you would never come out alive.

The Prince of Grenada was to spend the duration of his life in solitary confinement in a small cell. He was given one book to read the entire time. This book was the Bible. Having just one book to read, he read it over hundreds and hundreds of times. It was a book that became his constant companion.

After thirty-three years of imprisonment, he died. When they came in to clean out his cell, it was interesting to find some notes he had written using nails on the soft stone of the prison walls. The notations were of this variety: the eighth verse of the ninety-seventh Psalm is the middle verse of the Bible; Ezra 7:21 contains all the letters of the alphabet except the letter "J"; the ninth verse of the eighth chapter of Esther is the longest verse in the Bible; no word or name of more than six syllables can be found in the Bible.

When Scot Udell originally noted these facts in an article in _Psychology Today_, he could not help but note that here was a guy who spent thirty-three years of his life studying what some have described as the greatest book of all time, and yet all he could glean from thirty-three years of reading was basically trivia. From all we know, he never really made any sort of religious or spiritual commitment to Christ, but he became an expert at Bible trivia.

—From _Hot Illustrations for Youth Talks_ by Wayne Rice. Used by permission.

SALVATION

"Jesus Christ of Nazareth . . . there is no other name under heaven . . . by which we must be saved" (Acts 4:10, 12).

When I was in high school, I went over to a girlfriend's house one day. Her father answered the door. I explained that I wanted to visit his daughter, and he proceeded to ask me a bunch of questions. I didn't understand what he was doing; I just wanted him to let me into the house. Well, after about three minutes of questions, which seemed like three hours, he said she wasn't available and that I couldn't come in. I felt helpless and stupid as I walked all the way back to my house alone. What he did was totally fair—at least to him—because it was his house. He made the rules.

One day you will knock on the door of God's house—heaven—and guess who will answer the door? You will be faced with a similar situation—trying to get into someone's house—but there will be a few major differences.

First, God wants you to come in (I Timothy 2:3, 4).

Second, He has told us in advance how to get in (John 3:16).

Third, it doesn't cost any money, and we all qualify (Romans 6:23).

The best part is, if you are the Son of God's friend, you'll get in—no questions asked. Your name will be on a list of VIPs at the front door and God's house will be your house. Forever.

Sean is a good student at school and hardly ever gets into trouble. He doesn't do drugs, he rarely ever uses bad language, and he's not in a gang. On weekends, he often helps take care of children at a local shelter for homeless people. Even though he's not active in a church youth group, he does attend church occasionally with his parents. Almost everyone who knows Sean speaks highly of him.

Is Sean going to heaven when he dies?
____ Yes
____ No
____ I don't know

How about you? Circle the number that best describes your chances of going to heaven.

```
1    2    3    4    5    6    7    8    9    10
Going to hell        Not sure         Going to heaven
```

What do you think is necessary in order to be a Christian?
____ Be baptized
____ Be confirmed
____ Ask Jesus to come into your heart
____ Believe the Bible is true
____ Belong to a church
____ Don't sin
____ Be "born again"
____ Repent of your sins
____ Love God and love your neighbor
____ Act like a Christian
____ Give money to the church
____ Believe that Jesus died for your sins
____ Read the Bible every day
____ Do enough good deeds
____ Have faith in God

THE ABCs OF SALVATION

Admit that you are a sinner and need a Savior (Romans 3:23; 6:23).

Believe that Jesus is Lord and that He died for your sins (Romans 10:5-8).

Confess (agree) that He is your Savior and Lord (Romans 10:9, 10).

People should become Christians because . . . (choose the best answer)

_____ they will go to heaven.

_____ they will have a better life on earth.

_____ they will experience the love of God in their lives.

THE LONG JUMP

Imagine that you are out jogging one day with Mike Powell, who currently holds the world record in the long jump. Powell's record stands at twenty-nine feet, four inches.

While you are running along, the earth starts to rumble. It's an earthquake! But this is an earthquake like no other. The earth starts to split open and suddenly, you and Mike Powell find yourself isolated on a small sliver of earth separated from safety by a deep crevasse that is exactly thirty feet across. The little patch of earth that you are on is going to crumble, and you'll die if you don't get to the other side. Things are looking hopeless.

The only hope you have is to jump across the canyon. Powell realizes that this jump is just eight inches longer than his record-setting long jump. But he decides to try it. He gets back as far as he can so that he can gather as much speed as possible. He gets into a three-point stance and you yell, "On your mark! Get set! GO!"

Powell runs as fast as he can and right on the edge of the crevasse, he kicks off and launches himself into the air. It's a perfect jump. He sails over the crevasse and lands right on the edge of the other side. His jump is an amazing twenty-nine feet, six inches—two inches farther than his world record! But unfortunately it's not far enough. He tries to grab on to the edge, but slips, slides, and . . . falls into the crevasse and dies. Poor Mike Powell.

Now it's your turn. You get back into a three-point stance and take off. Huffing and puffing, you waddle up to the edge, kick off, and jump! Straight down into the crevasse. You're dead too.

It didn't really matter that Mike Powell was able to almost get to the other side with a "near-perfect, world-record" jump. It simply wasn't far enough. In reality, his jump was no better than yours. Both of you died.

In the same way—it doesn't really matter how good you live, or how much church you attend, or how much better you are than other people. You can't save yourself. The best people in the world can't save themselves. "For all have sinned and fall short" (Romans 3:23). No one is good enough on their own.

That's why Jesus came. He is the only one who ever lived a perfect life. When we put our faith and trust in Him, and make Him Lord of our lives, His perfection becomes ours. He is the only one who can get us safely to the other side.

—From *Hot Illustrations for Youth Talks* by Wayne Rice.

"For the wages of sin is death, but the gift of God is eternal life in Christ Jesus our Lord" (Romans 6:23). What do you think this means? (Check all of the following statements that you believe are true.)

_____ Sin is what prevents us from having eternal life and a relationship with God.

_____ Death in this verse refers not just to physical death, but eternal death (hell).

_____ Everybody deserves to go to hell, but God is good, so He would never let anyone go there.

_____ No matter how small or insignificant you think your sins are, you won't go to heaven unless you receive Jesus Christ.

_____ If a sin doesn't hurt anyone, it doesn't really count against you.

_____ When you die, if you haven't committed too many sins, God will still let you into heaven.

_____ God sent Jesus Christ to die for our sins so that we can have eternal life.

GOD'S PERSPECTIVE

Read the following Scripture passages to see what they have to say about salvation.

• Romans 5:8

• II Corinthians 5:17

• I John 1:9

OPTIONAL ACTIVITIES

• Write a letter to someone, explaining how he or she can receive eternal life through Jesus Christ. If you feel OK about it, mail the letter.

• Try sharing the Gospel (the Good News of Jesus Christ) with a friend.

PRAYER

"Do not be anxious about anything, but in everything, by prayer and petition, with thanksgiving, present your requests to God" (Philippians 4:6).

Whenever I come home after being gone for several days, my kids jump on me and hug me. They bombard me with questions about what surprises I brought them, and if I don't have the answers they want right away, they run outside and play. They get excited about being with me just long enough to say what they want, but then they are anxious to go on with their business. I have to beg and plead for them to sit still and be with me for a little while. They are always in a rush to go play.

If they would only relax and let me spend some time with them, they would discover that I have some good things to tell them. They always have in mind what they want, and, if I don't address their immediate needs, they quickly lose interest. That's the way we are sometimes with God. We are His children, and He wants to spend time with us, to listen to us, and to tell us good things.

Whenever you pray, come with few words and listen to what God has to say. His plans are not your plans. He usually has a few surprises for you. (See Isaiah 55:8, 9.)

What do you think about prayer? Check the following statements that you agree with.

____ Prayer is good for you.

____ Prayer is basically a waste of time.

____ Long prayers are better than short prayers.

____ God only helps those who help themselves.

____ If you use flowery language and big words, God will pay more attention to your prayers.

____ It's important to close your eyes and bow your head when you pray.

____ Praying silently is just as good as praying out loud.

____ If you have sin in your life, you shouldn't pray.

____ You can talk to God like you talk to a friend.

____ When you talk to God, God talks to you.

____ Prayer is only a crutch for people who can't handle their own problems.

How often do you pray? Circle the following word(s) or phrase(s) that best describe your prayer life.

Never	Every day
Before meals	At church
Before a test	When I'm in trouble
At bedtime	Only in private
In the morning	Once a week
Once a month	Whenever I have a need

Complete the following sentences by circling a number on the appropriate scale.

For me, prayer is . . .

1	2	3	4	5	6	7	8	9	10
Hard				Not too hard					Easy

When I pray, I believe God will answer my prayers . . .

1	2	3	4	5	6	7	8	9	10
Never				Sometimes					Always

People pray for different reasons. Which of the following reasons do you think are best?

_____ To thank God for the good things in your life

_____ To ask for forgiveness

_____ To praise God for His greatness

_____ To ask God for things you need or desire

_____ To pray for others who are in need

_____ To spend quality time with God

_____ To let God know that you love Him

_____ All of the above

Which ones are the reasons that you pray?

GOD'S PERSPECTIVE

Read the following Scripture passages to find out what they have to say about prayer.

• Matthew 6:5-13; 26:36-43

• Mark 11:23-25

• Luke 18:1-8

• Romans 8:26, 27

• Ephesians 6:18

• Philippians 4:4-7

• I Thessalonians 5:17, 18

• James 5:13-16

OPTIONAL ACTIVITIES

• Write a prayer that you can pray every day. Decide on a time and place when you will pray it.

• Make a prayer list—specific requests that you would like to bring before God. Pray through the list every day and keep a record of how God answers your prayers.

• At your local Christian bookstore, find a devotional book that has some meditations and prayers in it. See if it helps your prayer life.

THE CHURCH

"Let us not give up meeting together . . . but let us encourage one another—and all the more as you see the Day approaching" (Hebrews 10:25).

When I was playing for the San Diego Chargers, we had very intense practice sessions. We spent most of our time, however, not on the field, but in the classroom. We had meetings for at least three hours, followed by our time on the practice field, which was usually shorter.

We had meetings for several reasons. One was to learn about the mistakes we made in the previous practice or game. We also received instruction. We were taught the right way to do things. Finally, we were motivated and encouraged to work harder and to do a better job the next time. Without those meetings, we would never have been able to play as a team, or to play up to our abilities.

Church plays the same role in the lives of Christians. The church provides a place where we meet together in order to know what we are doing right and what we are doing wrong. The church leaders ("coaches") teach us the basics, motivate us, and encourage us to go out and "fight the good fight of faith"—to win against the powers of evil. The church reminds us who we are, what our objectives are, and what our game plan will be. Just as a football team must learn to play together as a team, so must Christians work together in the body of Christ. No one can be a winner on his or her own.

How often do you attend church? (Circle the best answer.)
- a. Once (or more) a week
- b. Once a month
- c. Once a year
- d. Never

If you circled a, b, or c, which of the following words best describes your church experience?

Boring	Exciting
Interesting	Powerful
Scary	Emotional
Fun	Weird
Mysterious	Peaceful

If you circled c or d earlier, why don't you go to church (or go to church more often)? (Check all that apply to you.)

____ My parents don't go.

____ I'm too busy.

____ It's too boring.

____ I don't understand it.

____ I'm not a religious person.

____ I don't think it's important.

____ I don't know a good church to go to.

____ I don't have any friends who go.

____ I don't have a way to get there.

____ Other: _____

Do you agree or disagree with the following statements?

A   D   You shouldn't go to church if you aren't a good Christian.

A   D   There are too many hypocrites in the church.

A   D   It doesn't really matter which church you go to.

A   D   You can be a Christian without going to church.

A   D   The church is the people, not the building.

A   D   Watching a religious TV program is just as good as going to church.

A   D   People should dress up when they go to church.

A   D   Most churches are just after your money.

A   D   People who go to church are generally happier than those who don't.

What do you think is the main purpose of a church? (Check as many as you think apply.)

____ To worship God

____ To be a place where inspiring sermons are heard

____ To help make the world a better place

____ To convert people to Christ

____ To provide religious entertainment

____ To provide positive activities for young people

____ To help people learn more about God

____ To provide opportunities for people to serve God

____ To teach people right from wrong

____ To help people develop some close friendships

____ To help the poor

____ To produce inspiring music

____ Other: _____

GOD'S PERSPECTIVE

Read the following Scripture passages to see what they have to say about church.

- Romans 12:4-8

- I Corinthians 12:12-14

- Ephesians 5:25

- Hebrews 10:24, 25

OPTIONAL ACTIVITIES

• Bring a pen and a piece of paper to church. Write down what you learn about God, yourself, or other people. Write down what you enjoy about being at church or what bothers you.

• Visit a few churches in your area. Compare the various ways that people worship God. What do they have in common? What are the differences?

PRAYER REQUESTS

PRAYER REQUESTS